THE ASTROLOGICAL HOUSES

THE ASTROLOGICAL HOUSES

A PSYCHOLOGICAL VIEW OF MAN & HIS WORLD

Formerly titled *Man and His World*

BRUNO & LOUISE HUBER

SAMUEL WEISER, INC.

York Beach, Maine

First published in English in 1978 by
Samuel Weiser, Inc.
Box 612
York Beach, Maine 03910-0612

This printing, 1994

Special thanks to Haloli Richter (Lori Wallace) who translated this work from German into English.

Library of Congress Catalog Card Number: 84-51501

ISBN 0-87728-587-X
BJ

First published in German in 1975 by API-Verlag, Adliswil/ Zürich, Switzerland as *Der Mensch und Seine Welt*. Reissued in 1981 as *Die Astrologischen Hauser: Der Mensch und Seine Welt*. Copyright © 1975, 1981 Bruno and Louise Huber. Original English title: *Man and His World*.

Printed in the United States of America

The paper used in this publication meets the minimum requirements of the American National Standard for Permanence of Paper for Printed Library Materials Z39.48-1984.

Foreword
by
Noel Tyl

In the study of astrology, we astrologers easily become lost between the concepts of "what causes" and "what results". This dichotomous way of looking at life issues from a primal concern that has always been present with any record of human consciousness, from symbolic paintings on the walls of caves to the calligraphic symbols upon horoscopes, from religious philosophy to psychoanalysis. Man needs explanations of what was; he yearns to know what will be.

Within this thinking, a very important dimension is easily lost: in concern for what is to come we look to what has been and we forget about appreciating what is. We too easily project ourselves away from the present circumstances of our individual worlds and spend life anticipating new conditions. Lives become fearful, defensively routinized, empty, meaningless.

Indeed, creative preparation for the future is a wise attribute, and astrology is one of man's most creative tools for this wisdom, but man rarely gives enough attention to management of his world in its own terms. The wisdom loses depth; humans lose the texture of life's activity by neglecting to manage living as we grow. We project our human condition upon the planets, blaming them and fate. We forget ourselves and the world we live in every day.

For example, if two nations have a history of war between them, an apparent fatalistic strife, they have two major options for further development: first, they can project a future of continued strife because that is the condition that has always been or, second, they can come together to change the status quo of the present, to negotiate co-existence. By mangement of reality, by understanding reality's multi-dimensional texture, by exploring the actual world within any symbols or measures of deduction, the nations actively change what has been; they create new causes as they live and grow. Living knowingly transcends temperamental impulse and routinized habit. Levels of effect manifestation change. The nations negotiate with what is, and what is begins to change to what is becoming. The same principle can be applied between two individuals, between an individual and a group, between an individual and his dreams and memories, between man and his world.

The world of events that presses us in our presents is placed astrologically within the Houses. The heavens are brought down to Earth. The planets become abbreviations of different departments of living wisdom and as such take their places on each individual Earth-map as the gods of classical times stationed themselves with their heroes upon the battlefield. These gods of ours, now symbols of all that has been learned about man and seized by the awareness of the astrologer, give us infinitely varied energies that can not be ignored in the present by projecting them eternally forward. These energies give us the capacities to react individualistically to events, to give events of the present values for the future. Reactions to developmental tensions become the essence of personality development. To deny the now, the mirror that is the present, is to deny any future whatsoever and to seek a reflection without creating light.

Bruno and Louise Huber study the astrological Houses in adamantly practical terms. They group concerns within the human condition into dynamically functional units of understanding. Their fresh psychodynamic insights place man into his world armed with richly textured understanding and individualistically creative remedial options. The Hubers' penetrating study of man and his world uses astrology to delineate a way of life within the present. Life ceases to be a cause to be avoided. Life becomes a stimulus *we* can affect.

This book is essential. It is the freshest and most penetrating view of the Houses I have seen in the astrological literature. Its title could easily have been *You and Your World,* so engagingly personal is its psychodynamic style. It guides us another big step forward to what we astrologers espouse but easily forget: that life is to be lived in terms of creative negotiation; that, to a great degree, it is what we make it; and that miracles emerge only when we know our positions—and our gods'—upon the battlefield.

We owe much gratitude to the Hubers for sharing their part of the world of astrology that surrounds us all.

Noel Tyl

Authors' Note

Dear Reader,

It is a pleasure to introduce our research results in the area of astrological psychology to the American astrological public.

After years of experience in our Astrologie Schule in Switzerland and Germany and with our therapeutic practice in the Astrologische-Psychologisches Institut (API) in Adliswil, Switzerland, and in earlier years in the Institut Fuer Psycho-Synthese in Florence, Italy, we feel close to a "new science of man," one wherein modern psychological perception and ancient astrological wisdom are blended. We present our thoughts in a series entitled *ASTROLOGICAL PSYCHOLOGY*, in German as well as in English.

This book is the first of our series to be translated into English. In it, we introduce the astrological house system in its original natural state and transform it into a modern psychological thought form. From the house system, we deduct the basic behavioral psychological attitudes of mankind, how we react to our environment and how the environment then reacts to us.

The system of analysis we present proportions and refines psychological diagnosis and shifts mankind away from numbers and mathematical formulae into the center of life and cosmic occurrences. We teach a psychologically differentiated analysis that recognizes people in their true nature. An evaluation like "good" or "bad" is avoided on principle: we respect people's individuality and view them holistically. The synthesis of psychology and astrology affords a differentiated grasp of the personality as well as an integration and reshaping of the whole human being. This gives opportunity for the development of creative potentials.

We share with you the great depth and diversification of the twelve houses, or life areas, as a reference system to the real world as well as to psychological processes, those that constantly occur between mankind and each individual environment. We are all striving for a better understanding of astrology, of ourselves, and our relationship to the environment.

Bruno and Louise Huber
Adliswil, June 8, 1977

Planet Symbols

Sun	☉	♃	Jupiter
Moon	☽	♄	Saturn
Mercury	☿	♅	Uranus
Venus	♀	♆	Neptune
Mars	♂	♇	Pluto
Moon's North Node	☊		

Sign Symbols

Aries	♈	♎	Libra
Taurus	♉	♏	Scorpio
Gemini	♊	♐	Sagittarius
Cancer	♋	♑	Capricorn
Leo	♌	♒	Aquarius
Virgo	♍	♓	Pisces

Abbreviations

AC	=	Ascendent		HC	=	House Cusp
DC	=	Descendent		LP	=	Low Point
MC	=	Medium Coeli		IP	=	Invert Point
IC	=	Imum Coeli		GM	=	Golden Mean

Mental Growth: Super-Conscious Sphere

Creative Intelligence	Capacity for Love	Mental Self
♅	♆	♇
Uranus: Meditation Method	Neptune: Identification Comprehension	Pluto: Contemplation Metamorphosis

Personality (Ego): Conscious Sphere

Physical Manifestation	Sense of Self	Self-Awareness
♄		☉
Saturn: Practical Thought Processes; Need for Protection	Moon: Sympathy, Need for Contacts	Sun: Control, Need for Expansion

Life-Supporting Functions: Unconscious Sphere

Perfection	Formulation- Evaluation	Achievement
♀	☿ ♃	♂
Venus: Assimilation, Striving for Harmony	Mercury/Jupiter: Media Sense Recognition Mechanism	Mars: Motor Action, Energy

Drawing the Horoscope

The aspect structure is of greatest importance in the astrological-psychological analysis of the horoscope. It represents the consciousness picture of that human being. Deep life motivations, unconscious tendencies, inner life goals are visible in the aspect structure - especially within the spatial and timed positions with the house system.

That is the reason why we draw the horoscope differently from the usual picture. The aspect connections should be clearly seen as a structure of the individual horoscope. The ascertainment of the individual problems - possible for the testing psychologist only after many work sessions - is possible in a few hours with this way of drawing the horoscope.

The anglo-saxon way of drawing the horoscope with its equal house sections does not allow the portrayal of the true aspect relationship. We use the *zodiac* as the horoscope basis with the *360 degree* division. The calculated positions of the house cusps and planets can be drawn in a graphically exact way. Although the houses are of different sizes, the aspect picture is seen in its reality.

Below is our example horoscope in both styles of portrayal.

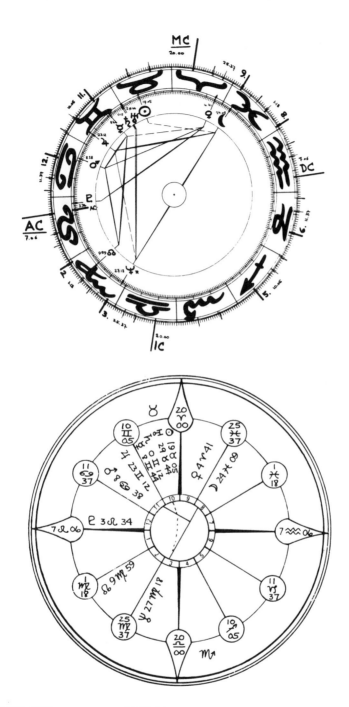

MAY 10, 1942   **11:30 AM**   **ZURICH, SWITZERLAND**
                                      47N22   8E33

In drawing the horoscope, we also normally use colors. In our extended teaching practice we learned that horoscopes drawn in color greatly stimulated analysis, and we recommend the following in your further study. The signs of the zodiac can be drawn in the four colors of the temperaments (elements):

red	-	fire
green	-	earth
yellow	-	air
blue	-	water

Sun, Moon and Saturn are best drawn in orange, to emphasize them as main planets. The others can be drawn in blue.

The aspects also can be drawn in color. We use green, blue, red, orange:

green	semi-sextile	30°
	quincunx	150°
blue	sextile	60°
	trine	120°
red	square	90°
	opposition	180°
orange	conjunction	0°

(We use only aspects of 30 degrees and their multiples)

Our color choice is founded in color psychology and corresponds to the aspect qualities:

red	-	active, tense, goal-oriented
blue	-	quiet, relaxed, harmony-oriented
green	-	undecided, seeking, informative
orange	-	contact-seeking, immediate, binding

Contents

Introduction

As is known, astrology can be traced back over thousands of years. We find fragmentary traces in early cultures, but its own system, a concept of astrology within an organized tradition, has been known for only two thousand years. In spite of the fact that astrology was not written down then, empirical knowledge was gathered through several thousand years. Uncounted generations of astrologers, including many great minds, have worked with this science and tried, through observation of man and his life, to find rules that were then passed on.

In this sense, astrology is older than any other science. One often even hears the argument that astrology is the mother of all sciences, giving birth to mathematics, astronomy and similar branches of knowledge which use astrology's mechanical tools and knowledge of nature's laws.

It is a remarkable phenomenon that astrology has survived to the present in spite of many attacks over thousands of years. Through the centuries, astrology has experienced great changes and development. From a simple ritual with magical images, astrology developed into a complex science. Especially during the last decades, with the enrichment of psychological findings, astrology has been able to blend with the thinking of modern, intelligent man.

Yet, we still have to come to terms with this long past, with this spiritual inheritance. The astrology of the twentieth century suffers from a certain illness which we can psychologically express as a special form of schizophrenia. On the one hand astrology tries almost too hard to be scientific; on the other hand, astrology in its traditional form consists of mythological and mystical images which try to explain things that cannot be causally understood.

Like psychology, astrology today suffers under the pressures for proof established by natural science and is lured to mechanical methods which are unfit for grasping human nature. That a humane science should be tested with the rules of a natural science is a contradiction and cannot succeed. Astrology must prove itself by what it is able to accomplish on its own terms.

Besides, we still have the strange phenomenon that makes it almost inadmissable, for example, to talk about the planet Jupiter without bringing in its powerful mythological colleague, Zeus, for the purpose of taking speculative Jupiterian qualities out of existing literature.

We personally believe that man's modern, logical and dialectical mind is not yet able to understand archetypal symbol-contents fully enough to translate them into operational analytical concepts. The instrument of our modern intellect, which is supported by and depends upon the process of objectivity, must under all circumstances accept a loss in substance when measuring symbolic results. The results we have had seemed unsatisfactory to begin with. We feel we must begin anew.

We put the emphasis on the recognition of inner-psychological forces and their vital processes in the horoscope and categorically deny the fatalistic thinking of determination typical of past centuries. After many years of practical research, the concept of astrological psychology was developed. Our research has oriented itself exclusively to questions asked in the practice of real-life therapeutic and counselling work, and not from theoretical questions typical in astrological considerations.

Each new step of realization, which resulted from comparison between the psychologically arrived at picture of the human being and the independent astrological analysis of the horoscope, had to withstand the hard test of daily application in therapeutic practice.

This process has led to certain corrections of the interpretation material historically handed down. Certain concepts had to be partly or wholly discarded; certain "rules" proved themselves ungrounded; new ones were recognized. Some concepts that, for centuries, were without foundation took on form and developed integral structure.

Today's modern astrological view is much less comparable with the vast variety of astrological rules of this century than it is with the simple, easy to see holistic view that shines through sources of early Greek or even pre-Greek (Babylonian-Chaldean) origin.

Research has forced us, over and over again, to keep out, to cut away, to go after the essential. The elements returned to the "essence"; there are now only 10 + 12 + 12 + 7 parts (10 planets, 12 signs, 12 houses, and 7 aspects) with which we must think. But we can use them according to our modern, intellectual equipment, finely gradated and differentiated. This will lead to carefully drawn, "point for point" verifiable character and behavior pictures of the individual human being.

We do not want to assert that the investigation of the astrology "instrument" is exhausted. Quite the contrary. But we believe we have found a secure basis for new astrological thinking that will stimulate further research.

With this book, we would like to share new thoughts on modern astrology. We want to talk about the human being, how he *really* is, how he lives and why he suffers. We put the human being into the center of life and cosmic drama, not numbers, methods or mythologies. We try in this first volume of a series called *ASTROLOGICAL PSYCHOLOGY* to explain the houses in their original experience nature. Intensive sense perception and intuitive recognition of the interconnections within the whole, as were natural to man in early cultures, brought the twelve astrological houses into order as a system of human involvement with the environment. With the development of modern, psychological thought formation, it is possible to understand and recognize the depth and implication of the twelve houses, or life arenas, in the life experience of man.

From a behavior-psychological point of view, the houses are the most important analytical element of astrological psychology. They are the reference system to the real world and they show the psychological processes which occur constantly between the individual and his environment. Therefore, we begin this series with the house system and not with the zodiac or the planets.

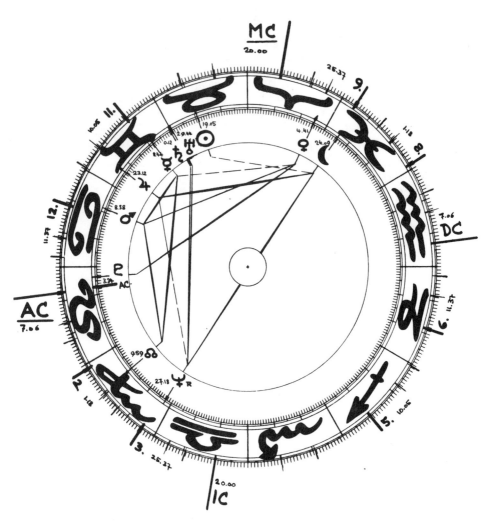

Example Horoscope

Name:

(Date) 10.5.1942	(Time) 11.30	S.Z.	(Place) ZÜRICH		

| | | | | N Lat **47.22** | | |
| E Long **8.33** | | | | | |

astrol.	Time:	23	30	· ·	AC	**7.06**	♋	☉	19	05	♉				
GT	(−2h)	21	30	· ·	2	1.18	♍	☽	24	09	♓				
LT	Place:	· ·	34	12	3	25.37	♍	☿	8	44	♊	♅	29	44	♉
ST	Date:	· 3	06	40	MC	20.00	♈	♀	4	41	♈	♆	27	18	♍ ℞
corr.			· 3	26	11	10.05	♊	♂	8	38	♋	♲	3	34	♋
					12	11.37	♋	♃	23	12	♊	☊	9	59	♍
LST	(−24h)	· 1	14	18	Tab.tg			♄	0	12	♊				DS

The Psychological Significance of the Horoscope

To recognize what positon the houses have in the over-all concept of astrological psychology, it is necessary to examine the horoscope holistically.

The horoscope, as is well known, shows the positions of the planets at the time of birth. From these patterns, one can extract individual characteristics and psychological developments through certain rules and laws. It is not yet understood why this should be so, but one can directly establish the definite operation of such interaction between planetary configurations and human conditions.

It is important to us that the horoscope represents the human being as a subjective center in his proper value-position within his environment. In this view, the horoscope is a symbolically translated picture of the human being and the world in which he lives. It shows the subjective view of man, i.e. how he sees himself, even if it may be mostly subconscious. The horoscope is the measure of his world, of which he is the center: it becomes then the symbol of his existence. For the astrologically oriented psychologist, the horoscope becomes an excellent diagnostic tool which can quickly and reliably establish an individual's problems.

In the example horoscope (page 20), we can grasp the whole drawing with one look. We have a graphic structure before us, which consists of different elements but which can be taken in visually as a whole unit. When we draw charts carefully and in colors, we can take them in with our senses. Then they begin to speak to us graphically. In the same way, we can view a human being standing in front of us, take him in with our senses. Some people have the perception to know rather quickly from the first impression another person's make-up.

In the horoscope we know five principle elements:

1. THE INNER CIRCLE; THE CENTER

When we contemplate the example chart, we can assume that the true essence of the human being is in the circle in the middle. This is where we look for the potential in man.

This center has many names. Some call it soul, psyche, anima or atman; others call it spirit, higher self or monad. In Indian philosophy, the life-giving center of man is called the divine spark or *fohat*. In the Greek and Christian cultures, we associate it with *entelechy*. In reality, we cannot describe and understand this essential core in satisfactory human terms. This is why we leave this circle in the middle open and do not draw aspects through it. The horoscope is written "around" this circle.

Symbolically, when man is born, the circle begins to beam energies in all directions, as you can see from the drawing. From this center, man grows into his world, to become and to be.

2. ASPECT STRUCTURE

The energies radiating in all directions first meet with the aspect lines of the overall aspect picture. This aspect picture gains very central meaning. It works as a basic "circuit plan" or a "reaction pattern" for the vital energies of the individual. Psychologically, it is the human being's portrait of awareness. From it, we can see the basic orientation that the individual takes in life. It shows the directions wherein his main interests and essential concerns lie, what he wants to make of his life (even without knowing consciously about it) and how and where he chiefly applies his energies.

Immediately, we can see from this central aspect configuration the potential talents that are within the individual, the ones that can be developed and used and the ones that will not present difficulties. We can also see the latent talents that cannot be expressed because they are not connected optimally within the "whole circuit plan"; they are connected but are standing aside, as are for example the sun and Pluto in our example chart (page 20).

3. THE PLANETS

The energies, which come from the central core of being, are transferred and distributed through the lines of the aspect picture of the planets, which are situated individually within the horoscope circle. The planets are the real tools of the core-being, abilities and qualities of a fundamental kind.

The planets are the *life organs* or *instruments* by means of which the human being makes contact with his world. Through them he perceives and experiences the world and establishes vital and functional exchange with it.

While the aspect picture is hidden deeply within the core of the human being and is difficult to discover as structured awareness, the planetary influences are closer at hand. Their effect can be clearly established.

In the horoscope, the planets are the most *flexible components.* They have different speeds of motion and are found in each horoscope in a different sign, in different distribution and relationship to each other. Their resultant is the differentiation of human character and the uniqueness of individuation.

Recently, a computer calculated how long it would take from one point in time to another when an overall planetary configuration would repeat itself. The number was expressed in quintillions of years!

4. THE ZODIAC

The signs of the zodiac connect us with cosmic qualities. They are the cosmic reference system, representing the laws and order of nature, giving to the individual "organs", the planets, a natural imprint. Only in this combined formulation can the human core energies confront reality and nature. Personal characteristics develop in the process.

In the signs we see the hereditary predispositions, the genetic structure, transferred to us from the parents, the grandparents, the race. From the positions of the planets in the signs, we can deduce through the specific sign qualities just which tendencies are inherent in the planets themselves, the individual functions.

The planets are "fed" by the signs. They are our *energy sources in life.*

Planets situated at the beginning or end of a sign receive less energy from that sign; when they are placed in the middle range, the energy flow is stronger. The optimal source of energy is in the twelfth degree of each sign (exactly 11°33').

5. THE HOUSES

The houses represent real and tangible life-situations and the areas of their detailed experience and activity. In contrast to the unique core structure of the individual (aspects, planets, signs), the houses are an *exterior*, not a primary influential configuration reference. The house-formation begins only with birth, and the individual deals with it all his life.

Man begins to live only when he becomes aware of his environment. That is why the house system is of such great importance to the consciously alive human being. It shows how the environment influences him and how he reacts to it (individual sensitizing).

When one is born, one arrives into a *life-situation*: first in the family, then in school one meets with a certain surrounding, a definite location, a social stratum, religious and political directions. All these influence the child and form its character. The configuration reference of one's house-system will be stamped into *behavior-traits* through the upbringing in the personal environment. The environmental factors influence the child singularly; it is being conditioned. The resulting formulation is a strong or weak personality, a strengthened or limited self-awareness, an individualist or a follower.

These reciprocal interactions between the central core (circle in the middle), the core energies or functioning organs (planets), the signs as cosmic stimulators and modifiers, and the different life arenas (houses), together make up the whole human being.

6. THE WHOLE HUMAN BEING

It is of the greatest importance always *to see the whole*. The inclination is to give more weight to the surface reality which is anchored in the character but is formed from outwardly influenced personality traits. It is easily forgotten that the inner human being is just as important, maybe more so.

When we analyse a horoscope, and therefore a human being, we must always try to recognize the whole human being, his inner and outer dispositions, his spiritual as well as his practical predisposition. Only then are we able truly to understand him and to give effective help.

The Astrological Concept of Man

A WAY TO SELF-KNOWLEDGE

The whole human being consists of different layers, from the center in the middle to the outer world. The most inner core-essence is very difficult for the individual to reach. Our consciousness normally is not in the center but on the periphery. We experience ourselves most dramatically and intensely in contact with the outside world. That is why we see our "I" always somewhere in the outside world: we identify ourselves with our reactions to the environment. Many sense this as determinism.

We can rightly say that through the environment, through society and its structure, through geography and its natural laws, through climate, through other human beings who live with us, we are influenced and to a certain degree "determined".

Nevertheless, we have the opportunity to ameliorate the degree of external situational constraint. But this assumes the recognition of the real structure of our Selves. This self-recognition is the pre-supposition for freedom.

Astrological psychology affords us a picture of ourselves, within which even our environment is represented as a potential function within our being. Through this tool, we can recognize how we are structured, including relevant portions of the environment. This knowledge can gradually give us more freedom.

When we study ourselves through the horoscope or through self-observation generally, the following happens: first we recognize the outer layers and their functions: that is, we observe ourselves in reaction to life situations and others in their reactions. We describe symptoms. They are contained in the houses, in our direct "correspondence" or "exchange" with the environment at hand.

This description of symptoms does not allow us as yet fully to understand our fate, to take it in hand and thence make it different and better or even perfect. But it leads us to the first step of recognition: with a gathering of observations, a certain distance is gained from the adherence to structured reality in daily dealings. We move, so to speak, with the planets in the houses back to the signs (de-identification from structure).

We gain distance from the formal reality of life and increasingly see ourselves confronted with our core-typical structure, which is not "outside", not in obligation to the world. We begin to see our *inclinations* to make contacts to this world. The distinction is important: through our inclinations, which are within us, we make contacts (bonds) with this world. This is the second realization that emerges. It gives us even more distance.

If we recognize our inclinations, which we brought into this life with us and which are conditioned by heredity and not environment (signs), we can go a step further.

We can deal with the planets and find out that there are abilities within us that exist in their own rights. Each ability has a function. Each has been tagged for a special purpose. Each is geared to certain possibilities. This deeper penetration gives us another degree in distance from the tie to this world.

Once we have recognized the planets as organs (Jupiter - the sense function, the Sun - self-awareness), we discover that they are arranged in a special and totally individual way. We all have the ten planets, yet they are in their total effect different according to the core essence of each individual, because the circuitry is different. We can see this in the individual aspect picture that represents the core structure.

Here is where descriptive astrology of the human being really ends. Only the circle in the middle is left and with it begins what we can designate as freedom.

When we withdraw through all these layers into ourselves, we see these layers from within as a transparent, complicated many-layered structure. Far on the outside is the world. Here in the center of the being begins freedom. Here we can say: this circuit or that reaction habit in the fourth outer layer is wrong: I don't want it. It does not fit what I plan for myself and my life tomorrow or the day after. I want it to be different. And from the middle I not only can voice this thought, I can also do something about it.

The will becomes effective here, matured through insight which is the result of introspection. It is a complex process—a process requiring much time and much serious and also cheerful willpower, to analyse oneself and to withdraw within. It is labor upon oneself that cannot be accomplished by pushing a button, from today to tomorrow, but lasts a whole life long. With a horoscope, we are ahead of other people. We can always re-observe the layers and orient ourselves anew in life situations, to recognize where we got stuck or were under pressure.

We can ask ourselves: where is the pressure point in this layered structure and where can we find a way out, a solution to the problem? Someone who does not know astrology does not have these tools readily available. We are therefore at an advantage which, at the same time, is an obligation not only toward ourselves but toward others. This obligation is also our spiritual responsibility toward the whole self as well as toward that portion we call will.

Because we enjoy the freedom given by introspective distance, we can develop and apply our will. One's free will develops in proportion to one's recognition of basic ethical tenets: how well that human being can harmonize his interests and goals with the best interest of the whole and how he can apply his abilities in that spirit. Then we are able to reach decisions which are in relationship to the inner as well as to the outer sphere of life.

First - and most important - we must deal with the central question of BEING in this life, with the meaning of our existence. An individual life needs clear and conscious motivation, to be lived fully and humanly.

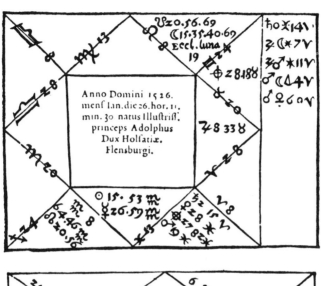

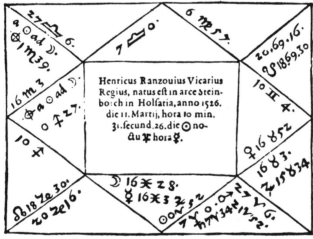

Solis.	*Luna.*
Declinat. v. 21. Sept.	Latitudo. 4. 14. Sept.
Afcens R. 0. 48.	Declinat. 1. 30. mer.
Diftant. ab I.C. 22. 9.	Afcens R. 345. 46.
Circulus pof. 28. 16.	Dift. ab I. C. 7. 7.
Defcenf. obl. 0. 58.	Circ pof. 9. 35.
	Diff. afcens 0. 15.
	Defcen. obli. 345. 31.

Two Horoscope Drawings from the year 1585.
(Heinrich Rantzau: "Clarissimae" and de annis climactericis")

THE HOUSE SYSTEM

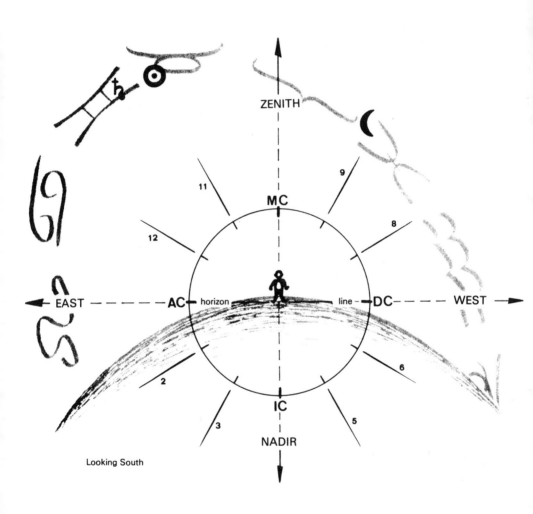

Looking South

Technical Specification to the Houses

Corresponding to dividing the circle of the zodiac into twelve equal parts, the ground and air space around the newborn is also divided into twelve sections, or houses. This "house system" is calculated not only for the time of birth but also for the place of birth as well (see picture, page 28).

A SUBJECTIVE SYSTEM OF MEASURING AND RELATING

We can see the star-studded sky at any time, day or night, from the place of birth and orient ourselves with this measuring system. It becomes apparent that the horoscope is a subjective representation of an individual horizon.

The houses are divided through the horizon line into *two halves*: the upper half where the Sun moves during the day, and the lower half, where the Sun moves at night. The left half marks the east, where the Sun rises and the right half marks where the Sun sets (west).

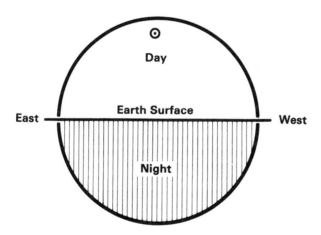

The Planets

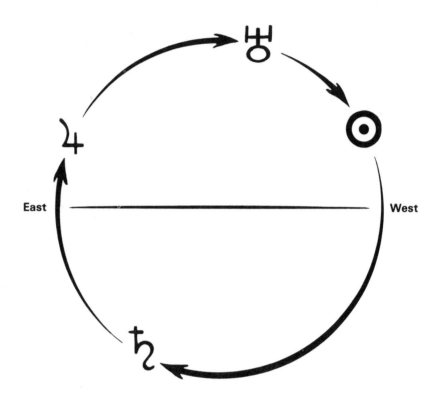

East   West

Apparently, each day the Sun, planets and signs, rise - subjectively seen - in the east over the horizon line and set again in the west. The Sun is always at a new position with every moment. If someone is born in the morning, the Sun will be in the east of the horoscope (left); at noon, high at the zenith; and, during the night, in the lower hemisphere of the horoscope.

The twelve houses establish the positions of the planets and the signs of the zodiac in relation to the horizon line of the birthplace. The point rising in the east at the moment of birth is the cusp of the first house or Ascendant (AC).

The point opposite the Ascendant on the western horizon, where the planets set, is the cusp of the seventh house, or Descendant (DC).

The highest point in the horoscope is the cusp of the tenth house. It is called the culmination point, the position where the Sun is found at high noon. It is the zenith or Medium Coeli, (the midheaven) MC.

The opposite point is the cusp of the fourth house, where the Sun is found at midnight, the lowest point in the horoscope. It is called the lower culmination point, the nadir or IC (Imum Coeli, bottom of the heavens).

These four houses, 1, 4, 7, 10, are the main areas, cardinal or angular houses of the horoscope. In between them are always two more houses.

THE ANGULAR CROSS

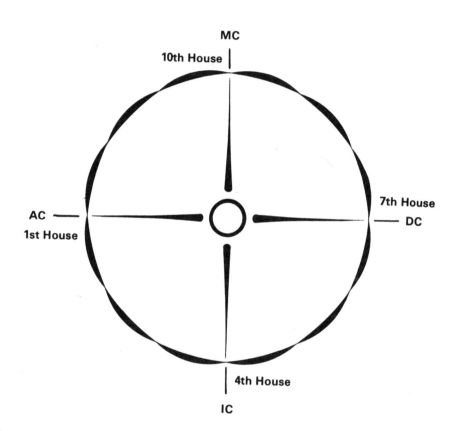

The counting of the houses begins at the ascendant, continues over the IC to the descendant, from there to the MC and again back to the ascendant. This direction corresponds with the rotation of the individual earth-horizon, which appears to be in counter-rotation to the subjectively seen motion of the zodiac.

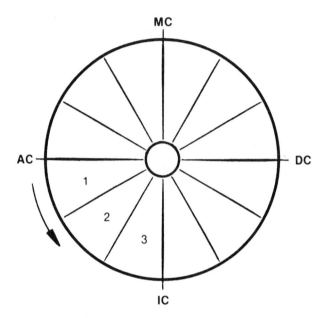

The difference and the relationship among the 12 signs of the zodiac and the 12 houses

| The Zodiac | = | cosmic reference system | = | universal or objective division |
| The Houses | = | worldly reference system | = | specific or subjective division |

As we know, the zodiac is divided into twelve equal parts, called signs. These twelve signs are sectors of an outer-worldly, cosmic space (of the Sun's system) and affect the whole earth. They have a rather collective effect, but they are cosmic qualities which are available as energy sources to everyone. The houses divide the worldly space around the native into twelve houses, and therefore have an individual and locality-bound quality.

While the zodiac is representative of all the constellations and oriented toward the earth as the center, geocentrically, the houses are related to man as the center, egocentrically. That is why the houses have such fundamentally individual expression.

We thus have a basic equation between the cosmic 12 divisions and the worldly 12 divisions of the house system. Each sign has something in common with the quality of one life area or house.

From a psychological and analytical-interpretative point of view, these two reference systems have a different significance.

SIGNS OF THE ZODIAC AND HOUSES

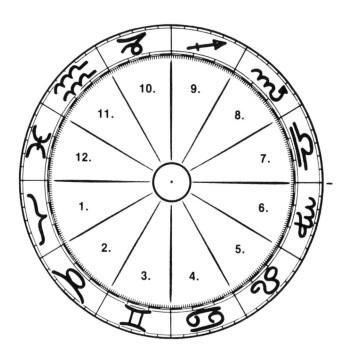

Aries	1st House	Libra	7th House
Taurus	2nd House	Scorpio	8th House
Gemini	3rd House	Sagittarius	9th House
Cancer	4th House	Capricorn	10th House
Leo	5th House	Aquarius	11th House
Virgo	6th House	Pisces	12th House

THE EXACT BIRTHTIME AND THE MOMENT OF BIRTH

As can be seen from the preceding explanations, the birthtime is as precisely necessary as the birthplace, in order to arrive at an exact house system.

Now one can ask rightly: who knows his exact birthtime and when is actually the correct moment of birth? There are three possibilities: the first cry, the cutting of the umbilical cord, or the emergence of the head.

The official birthtime can be determined by writing for a birth certificate to the bureau of vital statistics in the county where you were born. The birthtime is normally recorded at least to the nearest 15 minutes.

But the other point of controversy, which moment in the process of birth is the correct one for astrological calculations, needs further contemplation.

With the first cry, the newborn breathes air by himself. It is his first independent action and also a vocal and forceful announcement: I am here! The first cry or breath is the beginning of individual development. With the cutting of the umbilical cord, the physical bond to the mother is severed, the child leaves the protection of the womb. With this cutting, the independent functioning of the infant's organism begins. The first cry represents the moment of birth.

Until now, scientific experiments to find the medically and biologically definite moment of birth have not met with satisfactory results. The reason is that so far there have only been isolated experiments. Only research on a great scale will bring uniform results. But it can be assumed that there is a law in operation that we do not yet know and that must yet be discovered.

That is why we will have to work pragmatically in astrological psychology for the time being, which means we have to check the birthtime. For the general, simple overview of a horoscope, the official birthtime may suffice with its possible uncertainty. For psychological examinations and therapeutic treatment, however, a birthtime correction with life events is necessary (rectification). A simple method which we have developed, will be explained in a future volume.*

*Publisher's Note: The future volume the Hubers refer to was published in 1982. It is called Life Clock: Age Progression in the Horoscope, Volume 1. The second volume in the series is presently being translated and should be available in 1985.

A Fundamental Look at the Houses

The houses are the component most contested among astrologers and least understood by laymen, because it describes and includes the whole outer life.

Many theories exist: most of them are intellectual constructions that try to explain the whole matter with a particular system. But most of them get caught up in theory which does not prove itself in practical application.

There are several methods to calculate houses in use today. Some are based on Placidus (1603-1668), a few on Regiomontanus (1436-1475), while modern astrologers more and more use Dr. Koch (1895-1970). We use the Koch system (GOH) because its calculation to the individual birthplace allows precise and differentiated psychological analysis. The "age progression" is only possible with Koch-houses.

Actually, there are many possible ways to look at the house systems, depending upon one's position on earth. From each view, we can discover something new. Alone in the observation of nature, when looking south in the sky, there seems to be a curious "distortion" of the zodiac.

Only in spring and fall, or when we are at the equator, is there no distortion. But when we move north or south from this equator, we do not see the zodiac spherically, but rather "elliptically distorted". Therefore it is only our subjective impression, our view of the sky corresponding to our location, that determines how we see the zodiac.

Since the zodiac is the universal reference circle, the houses are also related to it. That is why everything is turned around in our horoscope drawing. That is why the houses are of unequal size while the signs of the zodiac are of equal size.

The horoscope, and especially the houses, are calculated precisely to the time of birth. The result is a subjective view of the sky as it existed at birth.

This results in the subjectivity of the horoscope, in the uniqueness of the human being who is born at that point in time, at that particular location. In another place on earth, the zodiac is differently distorted. This is demonstrated through the horoscope with its houses calculated for that individual. This is also in reference to the fact that each individual is different because he has been sensitized differently for this world. That is why understanding the houses in astrological psychology is the most revealing and fascinating endeavor and also the most difficult.

In astrology, the houses were always neglected, especially in the Middle Ages, because the psychological dimensions in the mode of thought were missing. Correspondingly, the keywords connected to the houses in the Middle Ages were simplistic and categorical.

1	Vita	Life	7	Uxor	Woman
2	Lucrum	Profit	8	Mors	Death
3	Fratres	Brothers	9	Pietas	Respect
4	Genitor	Parents	10	Regnum	Rule
5	Nati	Children	11	Benefactaque	Benefit
6	Valetudo	Health	12	Carcer	Prison

Through this mode of observation, the many-layered human life was reduced to few requirements, for whose recognition the horoscope was used. With those main concepts, the inner structure and connective dynamic among the houses were lost. Each house stood totally removed by itself, stamped with a rigid term, and had no connection to the next house.

A whole "catalogue" of single terms were gathered around each house throughout the centuries. This led only to contradictions, to confusion and finally to disintegration of the house system into single parts.

In real life, these life areas penetrate each other and are dependent upon each other. Influences of one house bring about effect and reaction in another. Each house is part of a living structure of life, within which the effects determine each other and intertwine.

THE PSYCHOLOGICAL MEANING OF THE TWELVE HOUSES IN DAILY LIFE

Behavioral psychological research has found that man is a social being and is mainly occupied with relationships to his environment, to live, to think, to feel and to act accordingly. He is not simply a product of a natural development but is also formed by educational, social, and cultural influences. We are born into a definite world which we cannot determine in advance. This world was built by others, through parents, grandparents, through whole generations and races. We arrive into this situation and must orient ourselves and adjust to it with what we bring with us.

It is therefore important that we know something about this world, recognize its condition, so that we are able to affect it positively, to do our share to make it a better world for us, for our children and for all.

The world always reacts back upon us. Just as we try to form our environment, we are formed by it. The movements are affecting in both directions. This play from inside to outside, from outside to inside, is the most important, the most interesting in life and in the personal horoscope.

The house system deals with this interplay. From the astrological point of view, it is the system of reference to the real world in which we live, to the practical and sometimes harsh reality with which we are confronted daily. It describes a whole spectrum of areas of our life and our interests in simple language derived from nature. These twelve life areas are the battlefields on which we fight, prove ourselves, struggle and work; on which we learn victory or defeat, depending upon our attitude.

Each of us is put into a life situation where we have to prove ourselves. We have a profession which we follow either as life support or from an inner calling. We have a family whom we love, maybe children whom we have to bring up. If we don't want to be alone, we need love and friendship. For our development, we need cultural and spiritual ideals, an atmosphere in which we feel at ease and happy.

All these are possibilities and realities with which we are confronted in life, which come toward us and to which we have to react in one way or another. Behavioral psychology and the astrological house system deal with these circumstances and our reactions to them.

Astrological psychology has the special function to point to the houses as the psychological life framework into which the human being, the individual, is put in relation to the real facts of life, independent of expectations and wish projections.

The Inner Structure and Dynamic of the House System

The following views have proved themselves, especially in the psychological analysis of the horoscope. They begin with the realities of life, put the human being into the center of cosmic and worldly happenings and consider both static and dynamic dimensions. Additionally, modern psychological knowledge is incorporated.

1.THE HOUSE SYSTEM AS STRUCTURAL SPACE

One can imagine that every human being carries about him an individual kind of house system. Naturally, it is not visible; one must imagine it. We can easily distinguish between above and below, left and right. Heaven and earth, east and west are points of view natural to us. But here we have to pay attention to the fact that the horoscope is oriented towards south, therefore east becomes left and west becomes right.

First, we always divide the space around us vertically and horizontally. In this way, the house system becomes instantly understandable to everyone. It is the experience of space in nature itself that allows a dynamic interpretation of man in relationship to his environment. From it we can draw behaviorally psychological conclusions with which we will deal in detail in this book, after the following orientation.

The four cardinal points	Above, below, right, and left
The cardinal (angular) cross	The horizontal and vertical axes
The Quadrants	The quadrants of the circle
The Zones	Expansion and contraction
The Polarity axes	The pairs of houses in opposition
The Intensity Curve	House cusps, "invert-point", "low-point"

2. THE DEVELOPMENT PROCESS OF THE HOROSCOPE

The House System in Crosses (quadruplicities) and Temperaments (triplicities).

The Three Crosses (the three quadruplicities: the cardinal, fixed, and mutable modes)	Motivation, way of thinking, attitude
The Four Temperaments (the four triplicities: the Fire, Earth, Air, and Water elements)	Quality of behavior, method of doing

Through the combination of crosses (modes) and temperaments (elements), a bond between the dimensions of space and time is formed. Growth patterns become visible, developing in a three-phase process.

The twelve houses are no longer seen as a classic space structure but as dynamic developmental tendencies which result from the combination of crosses (modes) and temperaments (elements), a basic three-phase development process, and as the tensions between ability and environment. These are developed in the following five points:

- The four development lines relating the temperaments (elements)
- The three-phase development process relating the crosses (modes)
- The three-fold division of the 12 houses into 36 sub-effect areas
- Behavior-psychological analysis keys
- Balancing and regulating the process between houses (environment) and signs (hereditary abilities)

The Four Development Lines Relating The Temperaments (Elements)

The houses can be viewed in triangular relationships. We connect in triangulation the houses that belong together temperamentally (Fire, Earth, Air, and Water elements). From the figure we get the dynamic development lines for each temperament and, with them, the four worldly efforts of man.

Each triangular group consists of one sign each of the three crosses (Cardinal, Fixed, and Mutable modes). Through the connection of the four dimensions of the temperaments (elements) with the motivating energies of the crosses (modes) there develops a dynamic development process that is connected with the transformation of the "I". It is best seen in the development lines of the temperaments that connect the signs within each element.

The Fire Houses correspond to:	1 Aries	5 Leo	9 Sagittarius	Personality development
The Earth Houses correspond to:	2 Taurus	6 Virgo	10 Capricorn	Social development
The Air Houses correspond to:	3 Gemini	7 Libra	11 Aquarius	External relationships
The Water Houses correspond to:	4 Cancer	8 Scorpio	12 Pisces	Internal orientation

The Three-phase Development Process of the Crosses (Modes)

To begin with, everything in nature, in our space orientation, is based on duality, on polarity. Only then develops a third pole: the intelligence that allows a development of the personality.

The concept of three lies always at the root, at the level of motivation or impulse while the four temperaments (elements) basically express the behavioral quality and method of the activity.

Each of the four quadrants contains three houses, whose significances are determined by the crosses (the three modes): first a cardinal, then a fixed, and lastly a mutable house. The first house gives impulse; the second fixes what is developing; the third dissolves it again and seeks something new. A new quadrant begins, again with an impulse.

The Cardinal Houses	1	4	7	10	*Impulse*
correspond to:	Aries	Cancer	Libra	Capricorn	
The Fixed Houses	2	5	8	11	*Consolidation*
correspond to:	Taurus	Leo	Scorpio	Aquarius	
The Mutable Houses	3	6	9	12	*Change*
correspond to:	Gemini	Virgo	Sagittarius	Pisces	

Division of the 12 Houses into 36 Sub-activity Areas

The three-phase development occurs in the quadruplicities in each quadrant, but also in each single house. That is why a differentiated judgement of psychological behavior forms is possible, depending in which section of a house planets are found, where life-forces are effective.

The first section of a house corresponds to the cardinal impulse, the second (middle portion) to the fixed, the third to the mutable, changeable. The result is 36 areas of sub-activity overall which are a key to understanding behavior.

Balance and Adjustment process between Houses [environment] and Signs [heredity].

The tensions between character and conditioning, between inherited traits and environmental influences, force the human being into growth, into changing and smoothing his character. The signs on the houses with the planets as life-forces will be reshaped by life, changed and clarified. Knowledge of the process provides important insight for the individual's developmental tendencies.

3. AGE PROGRESSION (AGE POINT)*

Age Progression represents a detailed contemplation of the course of life between 0 and 72 years or longer, and is comprised of time dimensions. It is a method of progression. It can be used to determine the present psychological state as well as future developmental possibilities and birth time correction.

In Age Progression, the houses are viewed consecutively: 1, 2, 3, etc, with each house representing a 6 year period of life and all 12 houses totalling 72 years of life.

* This was developed by Bruno Huber after many years of research.

Age Progression can be thought of as a time progression of the "Consciousness Focal Point" that begins at the Ascendant and moves with time through the different houses. That is why we also refer to it as the "Age Point".

This "Age Point" moves counter-clockwise through a house during a period of six years, when the psychological theme of that house gains important inner and outer focus. The houses or life areas should be understood psychologically as tangible results of the expression of certain psychological functions within the human being. These psychological energies are primary in the analysis of the Age Progression; the material manifestation or resulting events are secondary.

The obligations, problems, difficulties, timed experiences and events are nothing but the objectification of psychological energies, already present in the natal horoscope. When the "Age Point" reaches a planet, our "consciousness focus" concentrates on this planet and on all that it indicates within us in terms of opportunities, problems, and psychological factors.

In this connection, we also use the astrological color-circle, a spectrum portraying a cyclic course of life from red to purple, complementing the psychological analysis. (A detailed demonstraton of the "Age Point" will be published separately).

4. THE SIGNS AND PLANETS IN THE HOUSES

There are 12 x 12 x 10 possible combinations of signs, house qualities, and planets. This is a very richly textured subject and an important factor in analysis of character traits and conditioning.

Summary

The first approach to the house system is the cross-orientation of space derived from nature (above, below, right, and left). It is seen only in terms of space.

A further approach deals with the passing of time, the course of life, to be understood in terms of time.

In between these two approaches are the triplicities (elements) and quadruplicities (modes) wherein the dimensions of space and time overlap and indicate the dynamic development in the human being.

The last observation refers to the different combination possibilities of the static and dynamic growth-energies happening always in the three-phase development process.

The whole embraces the extensive analysis technique of the astrological house system to be discussed in this volume.

Rules for the Analysis of the Houses

The analysis of the houses should never be made one house at a time. It must be accomplished always in relationship to other influences from the entire house-wheel, the whole reference-system.

Many astrology students view the houses consecutively, all in a row, each by itself. We want to avoid this from the very beginning because that view fosters a one-sided analysis. We must pay attention to the occupation and accentuation of houses in the whole space structure.

Man quite naturally is interested in certain life areas and not in others. He does this in correspondence with the fact that some houses may have two or more planets, others none.

If someone has no planets in a certain house, this area of life is relatively uninteresting to him. In youth he was unable to get close to these areas, which stay unknown to him.

Every horoscope has one or more houses unoccupied. We basically do not partake in everything life offers. Sometimes a passive interest exists in such an area, but we have certain difficulties with it as soon as we are confronted with matters from the outside demanding our attention. That in turn demands a development above self-interests with the recognition of trans-personal goals that not only serve the individual human being, but the whole, the common good. Such development can greatly influence vocational choice as well as general education and life attitudes.

The different size of houses afford a further distinction in analysis. For example, there are houses reaching over two signs, when another sign does not occupy a house cusp (intercepted sign). The energies of this sign cannot flow into life. The house cusps or axes are the channels through which the energies are made effective in the environment. If a sign is intercepted, does not have a house cusp, then the energies cannot be directly effective, as well; the planets that may be positioned in this sign can not be made full use of to express core energies.

With such "intercepted" signs there is always some bother; they preoccupy us, even if subconsciously. We do not easily find a solution to the problems that are indicated through that house polarity.

Then there are signs that occupy two house cusps. Here the opposite happens. We can be fully active in these life areas. Depending upon which planet is positioned there, it can develop into hyper-activity, "to do for doing's sake". Then, energies can be easily wasted and other possibilities not recognized.

From the house system, we can also recognize which life areas give the best opportunities for vocational advancement. This depends greatly upon the dynamic direction of the aspect picture. It points often into one life area, into one space portion of the horoscope: for example, above, right, left or below. The house system becomes obvious through spatial orientation of the aspect picture. We also gain valuable insights as to the focus of the individual development; insights of prime importance in the analysis of the horoscope and in counselling.

One can imagine a house in which planets are concentrated with the Sun on the cusp. This would give that house a certain thrust into the environment. There would be more to win than lose. In the opposite example when, for instance, the Moon, alone or with weak aspects, is positioned in the middle or at the so-called "Low Point" (explained later in this volume) of a house, we can assume that there is more suffering than productivity, that the environment has a strong influence and a determining effect.

If, for example, there are holes in the aspect picture, open spots, then the outside influences can enter through the aspect holes into the core being. The individual will be made sensitive, open to hurt in his most inner being through the effects of the problems indicated in the corresponding houses (life areas). He is wide open to the influences and can defend himself only with difficulties. The protective cover is missing. This is especially so when the "Age Point" reaches these holes in the aspect picture, the open spots, the "structural tears". Then an incisive developmental crisis can result.

The aspects can represent a protection for the sensitive inner being. They can modify influences, can screeen and transform them. Conversely, square aspects can build a "wall" against the environment so that there is no way for it to intrude. A life area or house that is blocked in ths fashion usually will be closed off to consciousness. When there are planets behind that "wall", they represent a segregated and unlived part of the human psyche that is often the source of psychological disturbance.

The differentiation of life opportunities for the individual is founded not only in the fact that some individuals have less energy or vitality but also that these energies are not able to function freely or are partly blocked. They are exhausted on their way from inside to the outside within the system. There are many possibilities for the energies flowing from the center to be hindered or partly destroyed before they have a chance to be effective.

CONCLUDING REMARKS

Even when house analysis goes into details, we must not forget that the house system works as a whole. One can not lift out of the whole the Ascendant or Midheaven, for example. With some astrologers, the Ascendant is thought to be in competition with the Sun position.

As we will see in further analysis, the Ascendant as well as the Midheaven are each one of twelve comparable points. In principle, it is not correct to push these points overly into the foreground just because they have to do more directly with the "I" and individuality.

The Ascendant and Midheaven are not the "I" (like the Sun or Moon, for instance) but *representations* of the "I"; or better, they are positions that I take in this world from my subjective point of view. The Sun is the vital principle of self-awareness. It is the central I - function, while the Ascendant is the location of the ego. This distinction must always be observed when judging a horoscope.

The Ascendant and Midheaven must always be seen in relation to the space structure as well as to the neighboring and opposite points. The *I without the YOU* (with whom it seeks contact), the *individuality without the collective* (where it measures itself) stay sterile as concepts when analyzed without reference to reality, to the real world.

Aspects to the Ascendant and Midheaven are not drawn into the horoscope because the planetary aspect picture has a different meaning from the house system, of which the Ascendant and Midheaven are parts.

The aspect picture shows the inner structure, the core of consciousness, while the house system (and with it the Ascendant and Midheaven) represents the environment. They are two different systems of reference that only have indirect contact with each other (page 22 and 23).

If we were to draw aspects to the Ascendant and Midheaven into the aspect picture it would give a false representation that does not express the true awareness-structure of the individual.

Only in synastry and with progressions (Age Point) are directional or transit aspects to the Ascendant and Midheaven and to the other house cusps taken into consideration.

Detailed Demonstration of the Houses as Space Structure

1. ORIENTATION

Our whole orientation in physical space, and also in psychological and spiritual realms, is based reflexively on the concept of above, below, right, and left. The ways in which we think and live are tuned to it. We would be helpless and not viable without this orienation.

The house system is nothing other than a physical reference system with which we can orient ourselves in the cosmos and in life, in space and time.

For further study, please see the illustration called Quadrants on page 53. We can recognize clearly the spatial divisions with which we will deal individually.

1. The Angular Cross	I-YOU, Collective-Individual
2. Left section	I space
3. Right section	YOU space
4. Upper half	Conscious space
5. Lower half	Subconscious space
6. The four Quadrants	Impulse, instinct, thinking, being

2. THE ANGULAR CROSS - THE HORIZONTAL AND VERTICAL

The four Cardinal Points
AC - DC, IC - MC

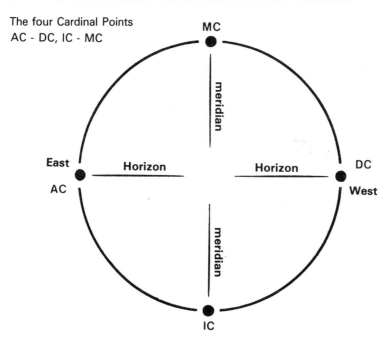

We divide the horoscope into four parts, easily seen in the illustration of the Quadrants page 53. This division gives us a cardinal or angular cross (horizontal and vertical). This is an important factor in astrology which we must always keep in mind. Everything is based on it, the zodiac and the house system. The two lines are natural lines, copied from nature and present from the beginning of all astrological thinking. This cardinal cross is the system of coordinates that gives us direction.

The division of the four quadrants had been changed in the development of astrology. At first, each quadrant was divided in two resulting in only eight houses. Later, about 2,300 to 2,400 years ago, each quadrant was divided into three equal parts resulting in twelve houses.

The quadrature is plausible and organic. With a little practice, we will be comfortable with it. We can easily draw that cardinal cross, see and identify with it.

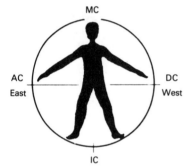

We can imagine a figure in a circle. The figure stands vertically and we see it from the back. The figure looks south. Therefore east is to the left and west is to the right; MC = head, AC = left hand, DC = the right hand, IC = the point exactly below us, the extension of our body axis down through the earth. To the left and right, the view is limited by the horizontal line from the Ascendant to the Descendant. "Ascendant" means rising, "Descendant" means setting. On the left side I see my "I", the portrait that I make of myself - *that what I am.* On the right side I see the "YOU", the environment and everything that is connected to it; everything *that comes toward me.*

The Horizontal Axis

This axis is the ground on which we stand and move. On a flat surface we can walk without having to look. We can concentrate upon the world, upon other human beings, upon the partner and meet him with the eyes, with the whole being. It is the natural basis upon which we function, live, and act more or less consciously. It is the plane upon which our life happens.

To the left is the "I"; to the right the "YOU". This axis is also called the *encounter-axis.* Each encounter with the environment, also with things and situations, takes place along this direction. The Ascendant and Descendant are two important points in the horoscope. On the Ascendant, we find our Selves, the "I"; on the Descendant, we find every human being we meet, the "YOU". Everything that has to do with human, animal, or other, viewed subjectively or situationally is played out upon this axis.

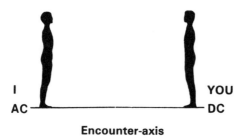

Encounter-axis

These contact functions are always in effect, as long as we are awake and active. If we passively drag our feet, we miss many opportunities offered by life; also if we do not ask things and people to confront us, to seek our attention and involvement, our reactions. If we want to be left alone and withdrawn, yet someone who needs us knocks forcefully at our door, or a situation demands correction, then we *must* react, if we want to or not.

We should try to get control of these functions, otherwise difficulties can arise that will lead to a contact blockade, especially if there are tensions in the I-YOU zones through opposition aspects.

This horizontal line can be expressed with the term *equalization.* One has to meet with the other on the same level, to find one another. If I put myself above the other, I will not be accepted because then I am already in the vertical line. On the horizontal line, one should meet as equals, as brothers, as partners, as human beings. We are dealing here not with a differentiation but with an equalization.

The differentiation that is made on this level is as follows: here I am and there you are. One is opposite the other. If we make too big a difference between the Self and the other Self, we draw a line that does not allow a true human encounter. We are building a barrier between ourselves and others that can be so high that we become disabled in making contacts. This is already a hostile act that will bring commensurate reactions from the other. Many times a refusal or aggressive rebuttal represents a drawing of borders. We complain about the other, that he does not want to have anything to do with us, but we forget that we had erected the barrier and that we have to take it down ourselves.

On the other hand, we can also pay too much attention to the YOU. For example, if we can not take being left alone and try very hard to get attention, empathy or acknowledgment from others, we will soon get on their nerves and receive a reprimand. Also, if we push ourselves into others' affairs, we must expect difficulties in I-YOU relationships.

These possibilities in contact behavior are indicated by planetary positions in the I-YOU areas of the horoscope. Details about these problems of this axis and their possible solutions are covered in the chapter "Polarity of the Axes" (page 81).

It is interesting that old house systems were based upon the horizon, while the new house system that we use (Koch) refers to the Meridian. The old systems aligned themselves mostly with the I-YOU problems while the new one directs itself to the vertical, the axis of individuation.

The Ascendant is also known as the "I" point; the Descendant the "YOU" point.

 The "I" point is the Ascendant and the beginning of house-division. Here is the self-image, the self-portrait: this is how I want to be seen by my environment. Signs and planets directly on the Ascendant have a strong effect and can be manifested in a special way by the Self. Conversely, the planetary qualities imprint the Self directly, giving such expressions as "sunny", "mercurial" or "martian", depending upon which planets are on the Ascendant.

 The "YOU"-point is the Descendant and marks the crossing of the horizon line in counter-clockwise development; the "YOU" comes into focus, is visible. Also, planets here give important insights as to how we see the "YOU", how it affects us and how we react.

Signs and planets in the area of the Descendant are a demand upon the environment; a primal, though often unconscious selective mechanism.

 The Vertical - Meridian

The vertical is the plumbline for us and is very important since we as human beings stand upright. If we would not instinctively feel this line we could not be upright. We would stagger and would have to steady ourselves continuously. Special organs in the body always tell us what is vertical. If one must be for a long time in a position that is not quite vertical, the body senses discomfort.

It is also psychologically important to live consciously in the vertical; it is the symbol of self-awareness. One who goes through life always bent over in a posture has a weak self-awareness. An "upright" human being will confront the world with self-awareness and will not be easily overwhelmed.

Also, by being upright, we have a better over-view. We want to keep our head high, as often as is possible. We can see much further and supervise events better. We do not like to lose control over events around us and be victimized by circumstances. As soon as we leave the vertical, we feel robbed of our own freedom and security. As long as we stand vertically, even if we have to fight, we feel reasonably secure; we still have defensive strength. But if somebody or something forces us down to our knees, then it is easy to lose self-awareness, crawl, and give in.

These are very graphic descriptions. They are vivid, and we accept them because they represent a deeper truth of life. It is quite healthy to be more conscious of the need for the vertical. We can do more with ourselves. Self-awareness gains a healthy "back-bone".

That is why the vertical line in the horoscope is the *individuality axis.* It starts at the lowest point, the IC, the background, the family, the collective, and leads upwards to the highest point, the MC, to conscious individuality.

The vertical can also be seen as a *hierarchical order* or differentiation. The human being grows from below to above and crosses certain steps, maturation processes, and social strata. A person who has this angle strongly occupied in his horoscope has the tendency to think in hierarchically discriminating terminology. He differentiates between small and big, rich and poor, between important and unimportant people, etc. The collective is an anonymous mass, and the individual is comparable to a mountaintop emerging from it.

Any hierarchical thinking comes from this angle. It results from the confrontation and corresponds to the need of the individual to stand out from the masses. Man wants recognition of his uniqueness; that is why he emphasizes everything that distinguishes him. Value judgements, status, and hunger for power can be tools of purpose.

On the extreme poles of the vertical line, we again differentiate two points of special meaning. (It really is not correct to speak of points. In reality, we have "areas", and we will deal with this later in detail).

The Individuality Point, the highest peak in the horoscope is comparable to our head, where we are the most individual. Our thinking is active and we identify there with our "I". (☉ on MC)

Planets positioned at this highest point form our thought process and our individual characteristics especially. We notice immediately if someone is "uranian", full of new ideas; or "mercurial", transmitting ides, communicating.

The Sun at this point is a sign of strong self-confidence, a human being with his head held high, recognizing and managing individuation.

The Collective Point is the opposite pole, in the area below. Here are the roots from which we come, where we grew, the family or a bigger or smaller collective. (☉ on IC)

If we have the Sun there in the horoscope, we do not want to be singled out as individuals; we try to "belong" and to be "accepted". In terms of the quality of the planet or sign, we integrate ourselves, are subservient or rebellious against the collective and the family, but dependent upon them. We either seek conformity and agreement with others or we suffer under the pressure of collective standards, restraints, obligations and deprivations.

3. THE LEFT HALF - THE "I" HEMISPHERE

The "I" is the controling and regulating principle of the inner, subconscious functions which serve to sustain life as well as the conscious self-experience.

It is the inner space, the private or intimate sphere. It is I with all my physical, psychological and mental interests, needs, problems and joys. Here everything is related to the Self; the environment is measured, valued and judged. Everything has to be "cleared" with myself before I can turn toward others. I discover myself in my thought and reaction patterns; and I commit myself to them, consciously or sub-consciously. The purpose is always self-preservation and self-manifestation.

Planets in the "I" Hemisphere

The life energy symbols here can be channeled by the Self. They are useful tools for self-manifestation and self-experience. Planets in the left half of the horoscope point also to self-interest, to egocentric or individualistic traits, depending upon whether they are above or below the horizon. In the negative, we can turn away from the world, withdraw into ourselves, and punish the world with our contempt, but also live without joy and become unable to function. Through too strong an "I"-concentration or withdrawal, we are without living exchange with the world, unable to make contacts, maybe even despotic or shy or incapable of effective relationship with the environment.

But we can also be so secure within ourselves that we are strengthened against the assaults of life, against the demands of the environment, and outer events can not throw us off balance.

People with an over-emphasized left side of the horoscope often have difficulties in contacts with others. They cannot easily come out of their shells, and they tend perhaps to judge others falsely because of a too strong transference of their own values to others. They are capable of contacts but they shy away from deeper contacts because they are afraid of injuries to the "I" sphere; so they tend to be introverted.

4. THE RIGHT HALF - THE "YOU" HEMISPHERE

Everything in this hemisphere relates to the environment, to that which is outside the Self. Here is the sphere of the YOU, the other people, human society. We find here everything that man has made: thought systems, societal structures, social benefits, economic necessities, duties and responsibilities, behavioral norms, etc.

The "YOU side" also indicates how we react to our environment and how the environment affects us. It is the sphere of the horoscope wherein we meet others, learn to understand the world and its structure, adapt to it or reject it.

Here, we are mainly interested in the world and confrontation with it. We can be led to too strong an extroversion and, with over-accentuation, to alienation from the Self.

Planets on the "You-side" are concentrated on others. Through them we can come into contact with the world, give attention to the other world, or conversely, with tension aspects or planets, suffer from the YOU. Here we come in contact with the inner workings of the world, with duties that we have toward the YOU, toward society, with joys and sorrows, depending upon which houses are occupied. We can either help others and side with them lovingly or we can reject them. We can manipulate and control or we ourselves can become enslaved to them.

A strongly emphasized right half in a horoscope indicates always how we react to the world and its demands. We can either fulfill them and be successful, or we can suffer under them and even be broken apart.

We can recognize all this from the positions of the planets on the "YOU-side" of the horoscope. They indicate in which ways we will try to affect the environment and, also, how we are influenced and formed by it or even become its product.   '

5. THE LOWER HALF - THE SUBCONSCIOUS HEMISPHERE

Here, the impulse and instinct mechanisms are active; they function without our effort, without conscious direction. In astrology as in psychology, we make the same distinction between conscious and sub-conscious functioning. In the sphere below the horizon, we normally do not know much, often nothing at all. For example, we must learn that the earth is a ball and that the sky continues on the other side. In earlier times, the attitude prevailed that the earth was a platter, a bowl, and that the gods drew the stars over it. That was a very primitive view, and it continued until more encompassing knowledge could be found. It is the same with the sub-conscious sphere in the horoscope, about which we know very little. All events and experiences are stored there and sink into the sub-conscious and form their independent system of psychological mechanism and impulses that influence instinctively our actions (conditioning and automatism).

The Planets in the Lower Half of the horoscope are difficult to employ for our conscious activity. We react to them mostly instinctively or impulsively, in reflex. Often, we only recognize them through what we have actually done, through the results from the reflex actions.

We speak in astrological terminology about signs and planets under the horizon as "experiencing the self through activity". One acts and so experiences himself. That is why the lower half of the horoscope is the field of activity wherein we react deeply and reflexively, doing what we are told to do and what we have learned.

People who have most of their planets situated in the lower half of the horoscope, especially grouped around the IC, try to fulfill the need for security and safety. These are sought out in the family or in a bigger or smaller collective, within a community to which they are willing to adapt themselves, to recognize its structure and laws and shy away from finding their own way.

6. THE UPPER HALF—THE CONSCIOUS HEMISPHERE

Here is contained everything that we experience in life consciously, that we see and perceive. Here we are able to seize upon impressions immediately, to digest them knowingly, to plan ahead and then to act. The thought process is well developed and can function, deliberately establishing a position and making decisions. The will finds application; there is a relative freedom from impulsive, unfocused reactions.

One thinks about the world and recognizes clearly and surely one's own position in it. This allows the possibility to create a place in society, because one knows how consciously to come in contact with the individual or that society.

The "I" is self-aware. The "I"-perception is no longer dependent upon subconscious reflexes; rather, it is effective in the world consciously, confronting the world with self-esteem.

Planets in the upper half point to a stronger self-assuredness. They represent abilities with which we can consciously function in life because they are above the horizon in the daylight. We can plan consciously, think things over, and do something with care and wise foresight.

In the upper sphere, we find the theoretical portion of the horoscope, in contrast with the lower part that is activity-oriented.

If all planets are above the horizon, there is the danger that man gets caught up in theory, living only in an imagined world that does not correspond to reality. Even arrogance, conceit, and pride can be indicated by such difficult positions.

Strong emphasis above the horizon usually indicates a self-aware personality, wishing to stand out above the crowd in some way, seeking an independent challenge in life. These people find it difficult to take orders; they have their own opinions and, with them, the courage to step before the world and demand their rights, to lead others. Often they have a natural authority that is willingly recognized by others. Sometimes they are also presumptuous and tend toward discrimination against the rights of others.

The Quadrants

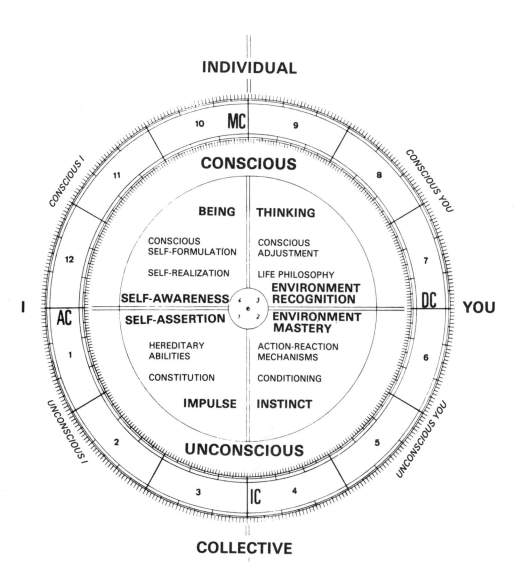

The Quadrants

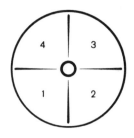

The angular cross divides the horoscope into four parts, bringing further refinement of psychological definitions.

The quadrants are theme spheres that give us a distinct orientation. There are horoscopes with all planets concentrated in one of the quadrants. We recognize immediately then that the main interest and also the best potentials on the whole are represented by this sphere for this individual. He functions and reacts automatically, most strongly and most intensively there. This does not mean that he does not function in other quadrants; rather, that he functions most where the planet concentration happens to be. There he learns most easily, can make the best of the situation and use his energies successfully. The quality - functions are different in each quadrant.

The division into four is extremely expressive. Even those who are adept in reading a horoscope should begin from this base and not go directly to planetary positions. First, one should always observe the distribution among the hemispheres, above, below, right and left, and then in the quadrants. This sets the main theme, the fundamental proportion to the whole.

Those who consider first the individual positions in the horoscope lose themselves in detail without understanding clearly if a given detail is important or less important, favorable or unfavorable. First, we should orient ourselves to the proportional distribution conditions by recognizing which planets are distributed in which quadrants.

THE FIRST QUADRANT   IMPULSE

Self-assertion, Heredity, Constitution
1st, 2nd, 3rd Houses

When we look at the diagram, we see within the first quadrant the part of ourselves that we do not know very well since it is under the horizon. Yet, it has to do with the "I," with the "I"-related world. This "I" lives here in the sphere of undifferentiated, impulse-dependent *self-preservation function.* That is why we see mainly in this quadrant the hereditary disposition, the constitution of the impulse nature. We see here how the human being defends himself against the iniquity of nature and the human environment in order to survive. Focused upon instinctive self-defense, he builds a security and defense system, observes and learns to preserve and master life. Life here is materialistic, self-centered, and defensive, and consists of objects.

The main motive of this quadrant is self-preservation.

The Sun or Planets in the first quadrant

They are predominatly directed to life-sustaining functions and activity-orientation. Impulses are strongly accentuated. This sector cares for our existance and survival. We must feed ourselves; we must defend ourselves; and we must procreate. These are the impulse functions that we try particularly to steer when the Sun is in the first quadrant—but that is not always easy! Over and over again we find out that we had already reacted before we were aware of the situation. The impulse function automatically responds in an urgent situation.

Such a Sun has more difficulties with self-awareness. It only recognizes after the fact what really happened. The recognition happens through the action. One learns from experience.

Further, we see that this quadrant is divided into three equal parts, the houses (in the outer ring). These three segments also have a special theme within the overall theme of the first quadrant. If there are planets positioned there, they are colored by the quality of these houses.

In the 1st house, we experience ourselves as the "I" with all its impulsive demands upon the world. We have a certain conception, a definite picture of ourselves, and we would like to think "the world is mine." We are here in appearance, a physical figure that confronts others, and we want to be respected and recognized. We try therefore to have a certain image, to make a good impression and change our masks often; we manipulate our image, our appearance.

In the 2nd house, we are occupied with the sustenance of life; we care for food, security, provisions. We acquire substance, talents, and abilities in order to apply them gainfully in life. Here we are possessors of real estate, finance, or mental possessions, whatever. Everything that has to do with life sustenance and life security is shown here. It is the house of economy, in the smallest as well as in the broadest sense. That is why we easily build here defensive walls around ourselves and our possessions for security. The "I" is lined up for self-defense; the self-esteem grows with possessions, leans on what it owns, including things, talents, abilities as well as other people.

In the 3rd house, the first contacts with the environment are made. It gives information about the relationships to brothers and sisters, relatives and neighbors, the near environment, one's way of thinking and mental attitude, the collective thinking with which we are imprinted from others nearby. We see here how we are trying to adjust to the world and, at the same time, to what degree we are influenced and formed by this world. This measure forms the collective, the environmentally dependent thinking.

THE SECOND QUADRANT   INSTINCT

Environmental Control, Action-Reaction Mechanism,
Conditioning
4th, 5th, and 6th Houses

The quadrant leading to the descendant from below represents that part of the sub-conscious that is determined by the collective and the YOU. We find here the conditioning formed in youth as a reaction to the influence of the environment.

We find the results of up-bringing and the influences of environment, our home in which we grow up, where certain norms and forms, customs and habits predominate; the teachers who influence us, the religious educators, the policeman on the street, the playmate, friends, the first love experience. Already from early youth to the middle of life, these are strongly felt conditioning forces that can be helpful or hindering to the predisposition of our instincts. Thusly, our behavior conduct in relationships is formed.

From these experiences and occurences develop sympathies and antipathies that, with time, become stereotyped feelings, concentrated within an action-reaction mechanism which acts and reacts involuntarily, reflexively and instinctively. This instinct mechanism gains form through our experience with persons with whom we come into contact.

Life is experienced in this quadrant as a subjective world. The basic attitude is offensive and emotionally accentuated.

The Sun or Planets in the Second Quadrant

Subconscious action and reaction dominate. We learn through experience, through close touch with the YOU. This quadrant deals with the YOU (southwest).

The inclination to contacts—even mental ones—is strongly formed. Interest in the environment is alerted but is in the main directed by the senses. A highly complex instinct apparatus, with a gigantic reflex mechanism, is operating, teaching us to react to subtle differentiations. We learn to use the tools of life, physical or mental ones. But we can get lost in the DOING and measure everything in terms of achievement.

The human being with the Sun in this quadrant experiences himself in the contact with the YOU. That is why self-awareness is so important. Correspondingly, an over-emphasis to the degree of aggression can be indicated.

This quadrant again can be divided into three houses.

The 4th house corresponds to the origin and source from which we come—the parental home. It is the original "nest", our conception of it, and also how our own home should be some day. It is the place where we grew up, through which our individuality and our character were preformed to a certain degree. That is why we speak here about tradition, the conservative attitudes, and about emotional family-ties and collective dependence. Here we also withdraw into our own home and private life. We see how we behave there, what relationship we have with our own family and the collective.

The 5th house is enterprising, ready to experiment. We want to test ourselves in close contacts and experience eroticism with all its hopes and disappointments. We want to gather our own experiences, to live and test and gamble. That is the reason why this house is also called the house of creativity, the arts, games, of love, children, etc. The fifth house serves essentially in the realization of self. From the planetary positions, we can see in which way all this is done: whether developed in natural self representation or through "impress" behavior.

In the 6th house takes place the battle of existence, the submission to life's necessities. Here we must prove ourselves, undoing unwitting mistakes of the fifth house or paying the consequences. It shows how we prevail, but also the defeats and the psychosomatic processes and disease that often follow, work, service, dependencies, efficiency and inefficiency and how all these reflect in the physical condition. Here we must find our "place in life", our "market position" in the work arena in order to exist in a way that corresponds with individual abilities.

THE THIRD QUADRANT   THINKING

Environment-Recognition, Life Attitude, Conscious Adaptation
7th, 8th, and 9th Houses

Here begins the ascent into consciousness. Above the horizon in the thinking quadrant, the YOU is recognized consciously. This requires *conscious* adaptation. It forces a confrontation with the YOU, with the human society at large. One is dependent upon the other and seeks a format for living together, a standard of values within relationship. Here we find partnership contracts, bonds of protection and loyalty, marriage and inheritance settlements; everything that results from and reflects the experience of interaction.

While the second quadrant is still formed strongly by the environment, stimulating our instinctive reactions, the third quadrant shows what we consciously try to do ourselves and how well we are able to measure up to the environment.

The keynote of this quadrant is the thinking process. Here we try to combine different concepts or intersts within one system, be it through contracts, ideologies, philosophy or religion. It is the area where objective laws, formalized thought systems or supra-personal ideas are recognized.

The Sun or Planets in the Third Quadrant

Here we push to win our place in society. Self-awareness is stronger; we can recognize our identity and therefore experience ourselves in contact with the YOU, with the world.

The Sun points toward the attempt of outward self-aware action. In order to create and dominate through personality, we consciously create contacts and relationships with society, to understand how to secure the right place in society. Extroversion of consciousness is the best key word for this quadrant.

In the 7th house is shown the relationship to the YOU. The "I" is directly opposite this area, the YOU, and recognizes that its own powers are not enough to master life. Here we want to attach ourselves to the single YOU, to move it toward a working partnership, to be sure of it. We strive for true partnership and must learn to subordinate ourselves to it. Frictions can arise because the YOU may point out existing shortcomings which are hindering a harmonious togetherness. We begin with conscious adjustment, through work upon ourselves, upon our own "I".

The 8th house demands accommodation to social reality, often bringing the death of old concepts or of a single, impeding commitment. It is also called the house of death, the die-and-rise-again process. We must discard everything unnecessary, all ballast, often through painful separation, because this is the turning point, a point of renewal of individuality's ascent while giving consciously to society that which rightly belongs to it (responsibilities). In exchange, we receive here legacies, inheritance or support, and also positions and honors from the YOU or from the community.

The 9th house is not concerned with acting but with thinking. We call it the house of independent, individual thinking, in contrast to the third house, the house of trained thinking. Here in the ninth, we want to find out for ourselves the solutions to the questions of life, to understand the meaning of life." We dare to cross whatever limits us in the establishment, giving to others as well goals and directions, enthusing them to participate in projects for the community or for idealistic purposes. It is the house of philosophy and worldviews ("Weltanschauung"), of education and worldwide relations.

THE FOURTH QUADRANT   BEING

Self-perception, Self-realization, Conscious "I"-formation
10th, 11th, and 12th Houses

In the last quadrant, the "being"-quadrant, we study consciousness, the conscious self-perception. Here we know what we are, who we are, and where we are. This quadrant is concerned with the self-formed "I", the conscious manifestation, that which we have distilled from life.

It is the area of conscious individuality. Here we can experience directly the "I", the Self, in order to view our own consciousness as a known quantity and use it as a measure with which to evaluate the world. Here we do not have an instinctive reaction to things; rather, we take in everything that comes toward us consciously, and try to bring it into relation to oneself. The reference scale is not the YOU, it is the "I".

Theoretical recognition, the conscious process, is naturally specially emphasized because it is free of impulse and instinct reactions, and it can move freely in higher, mental planes. Self-awareness unites within itself the individual and the universal consciousness and transforms this finally into the "state of being" ("Seins-Zustand").

The Sun or Planets in the Fourth Quadrant

This Sun position is best designated by introversion. The human being is not so much interested in the world as he is in his own mental qualities and abilities, in his mental interests. We observe ourselves, and we display a certain reserve; we only allow close to us people whom we can trust, who are on the same level and perhaps can be of use to us from time to time.

Here also there must be a certain self-confidence and the feeling that others can not threaten. Often we find with certain positions the situation of an "ivory tower" from which the human being has only indirect contact with the world.

In the 10th house, we want our place in the world. We want to be recognized for what we are and want to move as free individuals. That is why this house signifies the social position, social calling, or the striving for power. Here we find real or false authority, real leadership qualities or prestige, and egotistical power aspirations. This important position should parallel the degree of maturity of the conscious individuality and its readiness for responsibilities. Power pursued for its own sake will find here the just reward of falling from the heights, through loss of usurped authority.

The 11th house is the house of friends, of relationships by choice. Here we want to choose our relationships freely and are not driven by impulsiveness. We are intersted in the human being for himself and are able to love him without egoistical motives. The ideal human image as a model is developed, experienced in friendship with the individualisitic idea of a perfect human society. These ideas can also go too far: we then find the utopian dreamer who looses himself in unreal speculations.

The 12th house is furthest from the world; all the way to the left side of the horoscope, the last of the houses. Here we find the introversion, everything that separates man from others and leads him back to himself so that he may integrate himself in a higher spiritual context. Here we must acquire the ability to live quietly within the Self, even to be isolated, alone and lonely. It is the house of forced or chosen isolation, of productive or unproductive loneliness.

The Twelve Astrological Houses

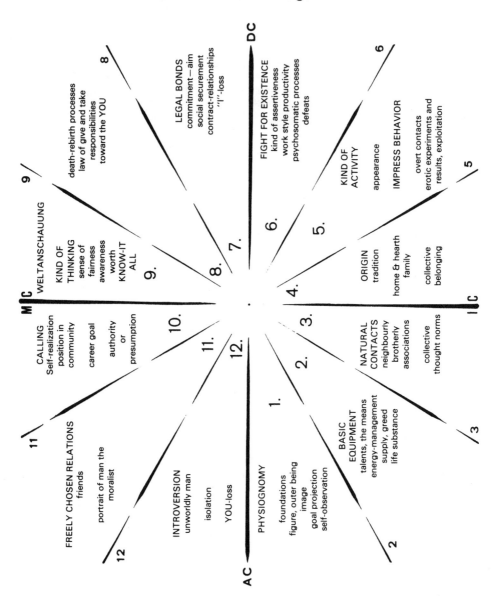

The Laws of Houses, Zones and Axes

Since the Middle Ages, astrologers have looked at houses as defined areas. If a planet is positioned within these fields, it will be interpreted according to specific house qualities. A further differentiation is usually not attempted. This is shown in the drawing (page 60). But it is obvious that the scope of a house and its influence area can not be cut off at a line with a definite border. In reality, these life areas overlap and interpenetrate to a certain degree. They have active and passive zones, zones that break out to affect the environment and zones wherein the environment affects the individual.

Some astrologers of the 20th century have discovered that planets positioned near the cusps (where a house begins or ends) manifest much stronger character traits than when they are found in the middle of a house. There were discussions for a long period about how close to the cusp a planet must be in order to be most pronounced. It also was not clear how to judge a planet as "close" when approaching from the end of a preceding house. Specific research was required.

We found after long and intensive research that there are different zones of effectiveness throughout the house system which, in detailed observation, provide a genuine analytical tool for behavioral psychology. A psychologically differentiated analysis of the horoscope became possible, giving special significance to the refined grasp and registration of the house system. With this fresh understanding, psychological behavior traits can be recognized, solutions to existing problems can be found in order to allow succssful application of personality forces in life. Since within the houses we can see environmental influence and conditioning and the mistakes that have been made in upbringing, we can also begin within the houses to see a regulatory development for solution.

THE LAW OF ZONES IN HOUSE ANALYSIS

The polarity forces   expansion — contraction

The reciprocal interaction of the forces of expansion and contraction, like opening and closing, concentration and relaxation, exertion and rest, are woven throughout all of life. From observation in nature, these two forces are as much basic attitudes and tendencies as are the concepts of horizontal and vertical. We experience the eternal pulse of life in infinite variations in nature, beginning with the life-support rhythms of heart and lungs. We find the same thing in the so-called "bio-rhythms" that portray the phases of high and low, of wave crests and wave valleys in physical as well as psychological senses throughout a lifetime.

Also in graphology we have the differentiation between the tendency for a script to lean to the left or right, suggesting conclusions about an introverted or extraverted character.

We find the same law applying when we view the space structure of the horoscope. Even with an empty piece of paper, we have an active-dynamic and a passive-static zone. Most people perceive the left side as passive, but the passive part does not extend to the middle of the paper but, rather, only to one third of its space, *to the measurement of the golden mean.* The right side, conversely, is the active one. In this measuring system, we also find a natural law and we will explore it more closely soon.

First, let us look for the expansion and the contraction zones of the horoscope.

The houses viewed in the expansive and the contractive areas of the horoscope.

For easy understanding, the drawing below shows a curvilinear contour. The curvature expands outwardly and then inwardly and therefore expresses positive and negative zones. Seen from the center, the curvature has its peaks at the angles (the expansive forces) and its lowest points in the intermediate houses (the contracting forces).

There are all together four trough-curves that include four houses and four crest-curves that include eight houses. We always have paired houses included in the crest curves.

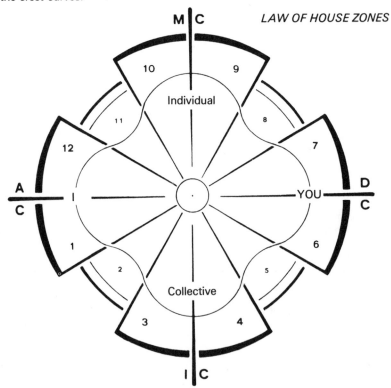

LAW OF HOUSE ZONES

Key words help us further in these observations. The houses or spaces around these two main axes are called expansion zones. Included here are the cardinal (angular) houses and the mutable (cadent) houses, building part of the cross: houses 12 and 1, 3 and 4, 6 and 7, 9 and 10. Where the curve swings inward, we find the succeedent fixed houses in the contracting sphere, houses 2, 5, 8, and 11.

This differentiation is important for our later analysis of the axes and poles. We will see that the houses in the expansive areas (the cardinal and mutable houses), although differentiated and obviously in pairs, are clearly in contrast to the fixed houses of the contracting areas.

In the expansive areas (which we can also call active zones) we find life energies produced. These zones are related to the Sun and Moon principles (cardinal = $\odot$, mutable = $\rangle$). We compare the contracting areas of the fixed houses with the saturnian principle: stabilizing, consolidating, limiting. In the expansive areas, growth processes take place; in the contracting areas, set conditions are indicated.

We now will study these areas and compare them in a practical way to life.

THE CARDINAL CROSS AS A SPATIAL EXPERIENCE

We begin again first with the cardinal cross that is the basis of all spatial concepts. We visualize that the horizontal line and the vertical line are not just effective as lines but as a whole area, an arena.

The "I-YOU" relationship does not only happen on the horizontal line but also *around* that line, above as well as below. Comparably, the rising of the collective mass-oriented human being toward realization of self-aware individuality does not only occur on the vertical line, but also to the left and right of it.

As already mentioned, the areas around the cardinal axes are the zones of expansion. Here is where important experience and development processes occur, where the encounter from the "I" to the YOU and the growth toward conscious individuality develop.

For a closer illustration we dissect the cardinal cross and show the houses of the expansive zones and their opposite poles.

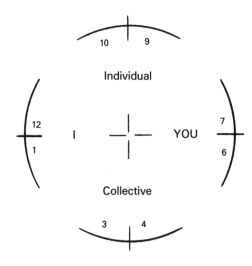

THE ZONES OF EXPANSION: THE CARDINAL AND MUTABLE CROSSES

For further clarity we arrange them again in crosses with the corresponding signs.

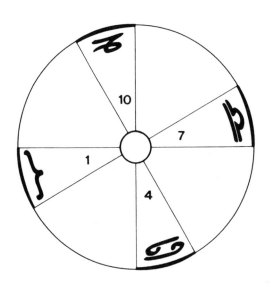

Cardinal Houses

1. Aries
4. Cancer
7. Libra
10. Capricorn

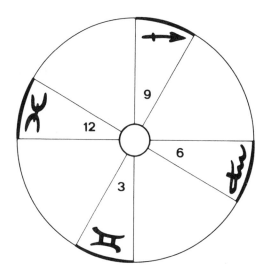

Mutable Houses

3. Gemini
6. Virgo
9. Sagittarius
12. Pisces

As you can see, both the cardinal and the mutable crosses belong to the expansion zones. They have in common the *dynamic principle*. But each of these crosses has a different motivating force. The cardinal houses have basically an extraverted attitude concentrated on activity. The mutable houses are more introverted, tending toward passive experiencing.

In the *cardinal* houses, we have the forces of action. Something is being done, produced, created, that later can be exploited. That is the sense of all the cardinal houses. Natually, these action processes concern different areas of interest and take on quite different appearances according to the quadrant in which the house is found.

In the *mutable* houses we have the forces of realization or recognition; processes of consciousness. Here we gather experience, criticize the existing, suffer defeats, part from the status quo, seek new and better ideas. In these houses, we always find the processes of recognition, be they enforcedly passive or actively seeking.

But in both groups of houses the objective is the life growth process, either active or passive. We can phrase it contrastingly by saying that the cardinal houses are the active ones and the mutable houses are the reactive ones. Before all cardinal houses, we find mutable houses, which clearly corroborates that thinking should precede action.

In the astrology of antiquity, these truths were already recognized. In the Middle Ages, the cardinal houses were called rising, determining houses, while the houses before the axes, the mutable ones were called falling or unstable houses. Unfortunately, these latter labels have become negative value judgements since things were often categorized into black or white, good or bad, in past ages. "Falling" or unstable houses are not bad or negative but simply outwardly not especially effective houses. They are passive, waiting, thoughtful. That in the Middle Ages particularly these mutable houses were underestimated is surprising since, in those times, "turning inward" was a strong dynamic of the era. At any rate apparently, what was outwardly effective and successful was what was impressive.

THE FOUR SPHERES OF EXPANSION

"I"-sphere, YOU-sphere, Collective-sphere, Individual-sphere

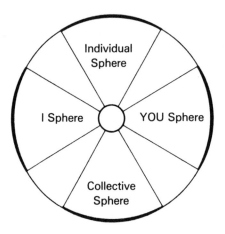

With the cardinal points AC, IC, DC, MC we also have a spherical effect. Here also it is not only a point that is effective but the areas left and right of the corresponding zones.

We can clearly differentiate these areas, and it is meaningful if a planet is in the passive or in the active area of a cardinal angle.

The "I"-sphere (or "I"-zone)

12th and 1st houses
(Pisces)   (Aries)

In the case of the *"I"-sphere*, it is not only the 1st house that is involved with the I but also the 12th house. In the 1st house, the "I" wants to be actively at work; the 12th house works with the same intensity on the "I", only in a totally different fashion.

The 12th house is a passive area. It is not overtly active. Here we lean toward observation, consideration, criticism. It is an area of reflection, of recognition.

Since it is part of the "I"-sphere we reflect about our "I". We are alone unto ourselves and observe ourselves. It is the quietest corner of the horoscope. Some of us do not like this area because reflecting upon the self can be quite painful.

Above all, the 12th house seeks recognition of the inner core and the reason for existence. People who are extremely extraverted have great difficulties with this area because it is so far removed from the outside activity and, in fact, goes over to the spiritual, transcendental dimension.

With the Sun in the 12th house, we like self-preoccupation. We withdraw and prefer to watch life go by from a distance. We tend toward contemplation, toward self-withdrawal, toward an inner participation rather than toward an external experience. Here we do not have big ambitions to participate in the "hustle of the world"; we keep at a safe distance, seek our own inner depths, and think about life and *Being.*

Should the Sun occupy an active, fiery sign, then it becomes difficult to achieve development in the withdrawn atmosphere of the 12th house. We feel excluded from life, misunderstood by others; we suffer frequently from non-acceptance or not being understood. The dynamic and vital forces can not become fully effective in life and, if we do not find the entrance to the spiritual world, then these energies will seek another outlet which can lead to psychological and sociological mis-development.

The 1st house begins with the Ascendant, the "I"-point. The "I" is involved in activity. There is not much contemplation, reflection upon the "I", but something is actually done in relation to the "I". In the 1st house it is a pleasure to imagine ourselves in an impressive role, and we paint mental pictures about how we master with ease the most difficult situations in life.

The Sun in the 1st house almost always indicates a strong personality, an imposing and forceful "I"-awareness that strongly attracts others. The vital "I"-forces of the 1st house combine with the self-awareness of the Sun and reinforce a self-assured presence. With the Sun in the 1st house, we are noticed by others; they do not pass us by but are aware of us. We are successful in life and make sure that our wishes are recognised. We work on our own "I"-picture and build up an image to show the world all we know, how good, efficient and sympatico we are.

In the "I"-sphere of the 1st house we see the world through our own eyes and are surprised when others do not react in the same way as we. We believe that others think as we do and are disappointed when reality does not comply.

The 1st house is there to show off the "I". It can also be the house that indicates if we really show our real selves or if we wear a mask that is not congruent with our real self but is meant to create a certain desirable effect on the environment. It therefore can also be an area of deception; mainly self-deception. This depends upon the planets in and the sign on the 1st house. But it can be the area where we show our real selves openly and honestly to the world and the YOU.

If someone has the Sun on the 12th house side of the Ascendant (within the Ascendant sign), then he still feels the desire to succeed as "I" in the world, but with placement *before the angle,* in the "shadow of the angle", the desire has difficulties working out. The attempt to draw attention to the self is not taken seriously. The Sun, the self-awareness, does not gain the attention as well as the Sun positioned *after the angle.*

That is the "I"-sphere. To repeat: on the passive side (before the AC) we are forced to think about ourselves; on the active side (after the AC) we can build an image and assert the personality.

The YOU-sphere

6th and 7th houses
(Virgo)   (Libra)

This YOU-sphere is opposite the "I"-sphere. Again we make the distinction of a passive, observing, reflecting house and an active house.

In the YOU-sphere, we want to recognize the YOU as it is. It is important to establish the best relationship with the YOU. This is the intent of these two houses.

In the 6th house we try to recognise how the YOU behaves when we present ourselves. We can observe here the effect of our 1st house: the 6th is opposite the 1st as houses just below the horizon.

In the 6th house we often are not so successful in contacts as we are in the 7th house. It is first a process of recognition. When we want to get closer to the YOU, we must first know ourselves. If we deceive ourselves and others we will not get to the YOU. The others recognise before we do when we try to deceive ourselves, when we are less than candid with ourselves. When we are unfit, when we behave unpleasantly, when we ask too much of the YOU, when we come *into conflict* with the YOU, we will be rejected. When we politely ask, when we have something to offer, then we will be more successful with the 6th house. We must orient ourselves to the house directly opposite, the 12th house. This means that our self-evaluation must be self-critical and honest in order to be accepted by the YOU. But if we insist on the 1st house, if we pound on the "I", then the difficulties begin.

The Sun in the 6th house demands continuous spiritual-mental verification. Here we must show what we can do and what we can give. It is a serving house. We will only receive something from the YOU when we have given something. Most often we *are* willing to serve the YOU, the other human being. Depending on the sign quality and aspects, this tendency can be extreme. One is degraded to a servant and never receives what one deserves. Service can not become servility, or exploitation by the environment will be the result.

The 6th house represents the coping with existence, effort, work, thoroughness and helpfulness.

In the 7th house, the active YOU-house (cardinal) we don't knock on the door as in the 6th house and ask: "May I come in; is it alright that I want something from you?" Here, we do come in and, depending on the planets and sign, we say openly and clearly, sometimes provokingly, exactly what we want from the YOU.

The 7th house is determined to create a functionally efficient relationship. We try to enter a relationship with the YOU in which each clearly states what he wants. A kind of deal is made. We confer, make agreements and put them in writing to have the security that they will be met.

It is important with the YOU to have an arrangement upon which we can depend. It is an active process to create relationships that have a certain form, a mutual legality. This is true partnership, the reason why the 7th house is also called the partnership house.

The Sun in the 7th house means that the YOU and the relationship with the YOU is important to the self-awareness. We experience the self most often in contact with others. One's own "I" is projected into others, and we expect the appropriate reaction, an answer from the YOU, from the partner. If the partner does not react with the right answer, then he is manipulated until he reacts in the expected way. We try to affect others with the whole being and appear therefore convincing. Someone with the Sun in the 7th house will always attempt an intensive exchange with the YOU and can contribute many vital life energies to the YOU.

We will act in accord with relevant planetary placements in contact with the YOU. For example, with Jupiter in the 7th house, we will want to be helpful to the YOU, we would want the opportunity to liberate the YOU from difficult situations. With Mars there, we will activate the YOU toward achievements, toward teamwork. With Venus, we will be charming, helpful and also compliant because we always seek harmony . . . and so on.

The Collective-sphere

3rd and 4th houses
(Gemini)   (Cancer)

The collective sphere comprises the roots, the fertile soil from which we grow. In the 3rd house it is a passive absorption of all existent thought formations; in the 4th house it is an intuitive feeling of security within the collective. Here is our natural shared heritage upon which we are mentally and emotionally dependent. *It is the sphere of active and passive belonging.*

The collective sphere is also an *archetypal sphere* belonging to the collective unconscious. In the unconscious we are permeated with the archetypal symbols and thought forms. Overlying this is generally a superstructure of collective thoughtforms which are formed through upbringing, the parents, education, and the public opinion.

From the depth of our being, from down deep, we know how something really should be. When the superstructure teaches otherwise, i.e., for economic or politic reasons or because some authority says so, then we must either stand up against collective opinion or repress our subconscious and "go against our better judgement".

What comes from the subconscious are always natural opinions, perfectly organic, that are not in discrepancy with natural law. Such structures are in harmony with the collective-unconscious and are not disturbances of personality development. On the other hand, collective thinking like public opinions or fashion trends can overlie the inner knowledge and hinder independent thinking. This occurs much more often than we realize.

An example: We have in astrology an archetypal thought form. We can turn to astrology for two reasons: first, somebody has told us that astrology is "great"; second, we can feel astrology's archetypal symbolic content deep in our innerbeing and identify with it. When I *reject* astrology, I identify myself with the super thought-structure, the scientific thinking whereby things that are not to be explained rationally are not to be recognized. Many people therefore have difficulties giving credence openly to astrology because rationally-scientific thinking overlies the whole and holds back the symbolic, ancient truth that sleeps in the collective unconscious. Conversely, when people do open themselves to this dimension of archetypal thinking, they then understand immediately what is meant by astrological symbols (see C.G. Jung, Volume 7).

The 3rd house is also the area wherein the collective thought formation and super thought-structures develop. The 4th house can lead directly to the unconscious. Here at the "deepest" point of the horoscope, especially in the nearness of the IC, one finds the archetypal area wherein man can return to the womb ("den Weg zu den Muettern betreten").

The 3rd house is how we think, the thinking we acquire in younger years. The environment in which we grow up influences our thought structure strongly. The habitual thinking of our familiar environments forms our own thinking strongly and colors it mostly unconsciously. We can scarcely argue with the basic convictions that are valid in our environments. This collective thinking has an axiomatic character and produces thinking habits of which we are hardly ever conscious. In the 3rd house, we do not think on our own to a very high degree; rather, someone thinks for us; collective measurements and behavior forms are determined for us.

If someone has the *Sun in the 3rd house*, he measures his self-esteem always in relation to what he knows and has accumulated through collective knowledge. He builds upon what he has learned and is always eager to expand his knowledge, to acquire a good education, to have good common sense. He turns with adroitness to those who transmit knowledge and could be useful to his own development. He always strives to show off his knowledge to others, to gain recognition and acceptance in the environment. His self-esteem is dependent on this acceptance.

In the 4th house, the Sun suggests a human being who belongs to an environment, not only in his way of thinking but also in the way he feels. In the 4th house, the feelings he has toward his own collective, his family, are very important.

The 3rd house contains collective thought forms: the 4th house, the collective psyche. The psyche is an odd and always variable mixture of thoughts, feelings, and sensations. One feels a group belonging. This is first a feeling and second a concept. We belong first as a child to the parental home, a nest from which we emerge to become an adult in our own family. The 4th house is the root soil from which we come but also the greater collective to which we belong.

This *belonging* is already there before we really start to think. As soon as we become aware of ourselves in puberty, we begin to ask how this belonging works and how we fit into it. Then the instinct awakens to go out into the world. This is shown at the top of the horoscope.

The Sun in the 4th house indicates that we need a home of our own. We are strongly tied to the family, the origin, and we feel secure in familiar surroundings. We have the strong urge to have our "own nest", possibly a house in which to feel secure and well. The sense of family and belonging to the collective gives us strength in life. But that means also that we may be tied to the home and not perceive the greater possibilities in life.

The Individual-Sphere

9th and 10th houses
(Sagittarius)   (Capricorn)

Here we try to find our *own* base in thinking, to be somebody else than originally conditioned. Here we want to fulfill our own individuality that contrasts with others through characteristics, talents, and thinking. This does not mean that we deny those others in our early surroundings, rather, we become differentiated from them.

In reference to the individual sphere and the related individualisation process Jung writes:

"Individuation is a differentiation process, the goal of which is the development of individual personality. The necessity for individuation is natural, while prevention of individuation through predominant or exclusive standardisation to collective norms indicates an impairment of individual life activity . . . Since the individual is not only a single being but also presumes collective relationships within his existance, so the process of individuation leads not to singleness but to a more intensive and general collective coherence (connection).

(Collected works Volume 6, Par.825, p. 477)

In the 9th house we think about ourselves and our lives; we develop our own philosophy, arrive at our own world view and our own ethics. Through it we can become something for ouselves - and in the 10th house also for others - an authority, someone knowledgeable.

If someone thinks a lot he has something to say. He feels the responsibility to find useful solutions for existing human problems, and he feels called upon to offer these solutions out of his own sense of duty and conviction that results from naturally developed authority. This authority has nothing to do with usurped authority that relies upon titles and names, that installs itself on a high rung but brings nothing along with it. Matured authority is not doubted by anyone and is not called authoritarian because genuine substance is offered.

The Sun in the 9th house needs breadth and space for self fulfillment. It is a symbol of philosophical thinking and world observation. Here we usually have our own opinion for which we stand up courageously. We identify ourselves with what we say and think and we impress others convincingly with a teaching effect. We can help with advice; we can find solutions to problems or at least view them from a different position.

With certain planetary positions here we are also dogmatic and announce our convictions with fanaticism; we want to convert everyone to our view. And always we seek consciousness expansion, though this may require long journeys or long and exhaustive philosophical discussions.

In the 10th house, we want to be and to live what we have won in knowledge in the 9th house. Through our philosophy, our realizations, and also all learned knowledge, we must express our own way and use it correctly so that the self-fulfillment which is always sought in this house can be achieved.

In the 10th house we must individualize ourselves and differentiate ourselves in our own consciousness, to reach an individual self-awareness. This is also expressed in achieving a competency through which the influence and power sphere grows. Here we identify with our work, which becomes a calling, and we achieve opportunity and self-fulfillment through a task for the community.

In proportion to how willing we are to serve the collective, we reach a position which is given by the community and which offers us the opportunity to grow above the masses, toward individuality, to become a leader of others.

The Sun in the 10th house is almost always a sign of a fully conscious personality. In any case, one wants to be his own person. With the vital Sun power there, one is almost always in the situation to achieve a position in life which affords personal freedom and opportunity to work out and up from the collective of the early environment toward a higher position.

THE CONTRACTION ZONES OF THE HOROSCOPE: THE FIXED CROSS

We recall in the drawing, page 62, the trough curve identifying the areas called contracting zones. As mentioned earlier, we always have with the crest curves two houses (expansion zones) while we have only one house when the curve goes inward. These latter houses are the fixed houses or contraction zones.

The curvature is in an inverted form in these houses; it moves through a contracting area, the fixed and stabilizing part of the horoscope. All that was created in the expansion zones is here stabilized and secured and passes into a solid state.

To repeat it once again: Contraction means crystalize, stabilize; preservation and securement.

We already know these terms from the signs of the fixed cross. In reality, these are the houses that correspond to the fixed signs and those houses we call fixed.

Fixed Houses:

2. Taurus
5. Leo
8. Scorpio
11. Aquarius

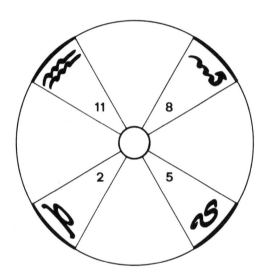

The Fixed Houses

We have the same basic qualities in these houses as we have in the corresponding signs. In these four fixed houses or zones of contraction no dynamic processes are indicated, no events; instead we have *states*, unmoving, stable states. When processes are suggested, they happen quantitavely, through repetition and multiple experiences. They relate to measurable amounts, tangible results that serve a certain purpose.

The fixed principles serve basically the purpose of maintaining, serving, and nursing, making something functionally useful. *Evaluation* and *application* as well as *perseverance* are terms that correspond to the fixed elements. Economy (not only in the material but also in the spiritual and psychological senses) plays an important role. People with fixed house and sign accentuation work toward the securement of conditions, to reach stability, to gain the security promised by the known, the trusted and that which is earned. They work so that all life functions are well organized and will run smoothly without the exertion of unnecessary energies. The momentum of this energy follows a law of inertness and accomplishes the greater part of its performance through routinization and automatization.

All that can be secured through planning and organization is accomplished in the fixed houses. This leads to success with relatively little effort when all that is possible is extracted from a situation, But it also leads to a strong tie to given conditions and therefore to a lack of freedom in the spiritual sense.

This subjection to circumstance or condition from which we want to profit happens mainly in all the fixed houses and, therefore, in the contracting zones, and plays an important role while at the same time being a weakness.

The striving for secure conditions is not only focused toward comfort but also toward an attempt to protect themselves from possible dangers.

The striving for security is underlined in all fixed houses. *In the 2nd house*, material security is most important; in the *5th house*, the recognition and securement of the personality sphere; in the *8th house*, the securement of a place in society; in the *11th house*, the secure organization and planning of relationships.

Someone whose expansion zones in the horoscope are emphasized with planets will follow his urge for freedom in individual activity. Someone with contraction zones in the horoscope strongly accentuated will try to order his life in a definite way. He will try to secure and insure all his affairs, try to live in the same place and be atttached to people whom he knows well. In this definite and limited area, he will do anything to maintain order. He will regulate and organize life well, so that peace and order will not be disturbed nor security endangered.

People with several planets in fixed houses hold strongly onto conditions that have been successful in the past. They are preponderately conservative and close to tradition; they are suspicious, doubting and rejecting in their attitudes toward the new.

It is much easier to create something new than to break up and change a crystalized condition.

Only when the insight of the mutable crosses and the impulsive forces of the mind become strong is the intolerability of old forms and conditions recognized and exchanged for new ideas. *This is why a mutable house follows each fixed house.*

Now we will study the single fixed houses, with a view to the "I"-hemisphere and the YOU-hemisphere of the horoscope.

THE FIXED HOUSES OF THE "I"-HEMISPHERE

2nd and 11th houses
(Taurus)   (Aquarius)

The objective of the *2nd house* is the securement of the "I"-sphere, the self-preservation and the assimilation of substances. We strive to procure the necessary means, acquisitions and adoption of talents, capacities and possessions with which to impress others and represent something in the world. All things that we can acquire, be they material or spiritual, belong to the 2nd house.

With the *Sun in the 2nd house*, we measure our own self-worth against what we have and what we can do. The worth of our personality and also our self-assuredness rises in terms of what we have acquired and achieved.

The 2nd house corresponds to Taurus, a fixed earth sign. Insecurities in the areas of possession, wealth or self-worth can hinder personal development. Difficult planetary positions in the 2nd house suggest a fear about holding onto one's possessions, about securing oneself against possible interferences (often without real reason); about defending and insuring oneself in every way possible. It is the house wherein we build "castles" for protection and defense.

Self-worth and self-defense are the two key words for the correct and incorrect functions of this house. If a human being is forced into self-defense and has strong tensions in the 2nd house, he will build around himself a wall that cannot be penetrated. He encapsulates himself in his own "I" (shell), goes into a "porcupine readiness", and considers other people as enemies, this can go to the extreme of paranoia.

Free contact with the YOU is made difficult because man is too aware of himself and his *own* security. If there is a close relationship to another human being, then this feeling of belonging can develop into possessiveness: the other person is held in an iron grip with no room for movement; he often becomes a permanent fixture in the life. Problems can arise here especially through the loss of such a person with whom one was in such close contact.

The same applies to other losses. They can so weaken self-esteem that trust in life and in one's own abilities disappears, and a new beginning is not ventured. This is why the 2nd house takes all precautions to avoid losses and to maintain the status quo. This results in a conservative attitude that often refuses change, but then again, it is especially out of this fear that we lose all we have.

The 11th house also involves the "I" but more in the sense of the personal characteristics that are respected by others.

If the Sun or an important configuration is in the 11th house then we measure our self-worth not by what we own but by the friends who must be special and valuable to us. We want to be with people who are harmonious with us and our individual development, people who stand socially and humanly at our level or higher. We want to move in the right circles. We enjoy being part of cultural, aesthetic and idealistic endeavors. Our self-esteem feels complimented when we are sought out or invited by others.

By identifying ourselves with missions or a progressive idea, we feel worthy, important or even better than others. Often we seek and work hard to promote a cure-all or spiritual teaching for the solving of human problems.

Here again, as with each fixed house, security plays an important part of what we experience in the 11th house, through belonging and togetherness with others who think similarly. We feel assured; our self-worth is elevated when we are part of something important that is being done for the betterment of the world. This can be accomplished through affiliations with progressive groups, society, or organizations, also through industry or in factories as well as in "high society". We will always work toward finding a place in a group, in teamwork with friends. We create relationships or organize groups in which we can play an appropriate role.

The essentials of the 11th house are the chosen friends, the "relatives by choice", the true and genuine friendships. The friend—the circle of friends through which understanding and secure rapport are gained—can mean so much that, often, other things in life are forgotten and other people are neglected irresponsibly. We may, for example, stand up more for our friends and groups and *their* opinions than for those of our own family!

Here too, we can find development mistakes and problems. With difficult astrological positions, we easily build fanatical or exaggerated concepts of the world and our friends. In our need for friends and for union, we can get with the "wrong crowd". We are easily deceived when we rely too much upon friends; or when we project our highest ideals onto them—if they do not behave as we expect them to—then a whole world breaks down, we are deeply hurt, our own "I" is injured, we feel disappointed, misunderstood, left out and rejected.

As a result, we lock ourselves up: we become mistrusting and highly selective; nobody fits with us, and we find faults with all. We limit ourselves to a few people whom we can trust and with whom we feel safe. We reject all others bluntly, become snobbish and arrogant or develop into an eccentric. The "I" is blown out of proportion while others seem worthless. An isolation develops, an "ivory tower", a blocking of the contact behavior, of course depending upon which planets are in the 11th house.

THE FIXED HOUSES IN THE YOU-Hemisphere

5th and 8th houses
(Leo)   (Scorpio)

In the 5th house, we seek to test and experience ourselves in the world and especially in close contact with the YOU.

With the Sun in the 5th house we are sure of ourselves and step before the world without concern. Here we seek contact with the YOU, we do not shrink from adventures and experiments. We have the courage to exhibit ourselves, to come forward, to risk and gamble, and we want to create a new world. Our creative potency and self-formation want to bloom and be effective; be the bloom through love, through art or through whatever in life we willfully chose, ignoring limitations and rules. Always it is self-realization and the presentation of one's personality, as we please, that is important. Our own projects and products (children too) serve that drive.

In the 5th house we want to be accepted by the YOU. We make some "noise" so that the YOU notices us. It is the "impress-behavior" with which we want to make an impression, just as animals want to lure a partner. In the 5th house we want to experience ourselves intimately with a partner. That is why we look for self-confirmation in eroticism, in love and its hopes and disappointments. Disappointments in love go deep, and if we make our self-esteem too dependent upon the relationship we will be jealous of everything that may interfere. We suffer from every change in the relationship, in the close contact. We possessively try to hard to hold onto love, and we must learn that this phenomenon follows its own laws, impervious to our manipulations of it.

The 5th house corresponds with the fixed fire sign Leo, and of course there is a tendency for security in all fixed signs. The security in the 5th house is sought in the definition of our own personality sphere, whereby even people can be part of our "possessions". If this sphere is assailed or contested, hard fights follow for the territory, for the sphere of influence, for prestige, for the area of competency, and also for the people who belong there.

Also, no one is allowed to interfere in the sphere of intimate contacts with others. The "intimacy sphere" is protected as untouchable territory, as a holy place secured against outside influence.

One's own self, one's own inner being is shielded from strangers' view. In the 5th house, we do not want to "lose face"; we must maintain dignity, taking hardships of fate proudly, with head held high. This is especially so, when the Sun is placed there.

With certain Moon positions, the 5th house can indicate developments where we want to remain as children and enjoy life and its joys in childish ways. We refuse to grow up or form close alliances with the YOU. We prefer to play rather than face the seriousness of life.

With Saturn in the 5th house, we are often afraid of real life experience, of experiments, of love, of intimate contact with others. We are introverted and miss or neglect our own development.

This can lead, depending upon planetary positions, to an infantile attitude, to repression of the joy of living, to denial of sexual instincts or to sterility and frustration in the erotic nature, with all the psychological consequences. These manifestations most often have their roots in a 5th house not lived or experienced.

The 8th house corresponds to the fixed water sign Scorpio. Here we deal with human society structure and its habits, laws, security tendencies. Here we are less interested in the single YOU, and rather more in the position, the competency, and the power sphere held in the world by the YOU. We are aware of what others own and what they have to offer. This includes material possessions that give others a secure position, as well as mental possessions, knowledge, experience and accomplishments.

The Sun in the 8th house almost always indicates an inheritance that we have to take over, *either materially or spiritually/mentally*. This is why we have interest in laws that protect against interference and encroachment by third persons. We promote these laws and the societal structure; we defend them whenever the opportunity arises and use them for our own gain. Through laws and rules, through cultural ethics and mores, we try to secure our own positions in our professions and in society, including individual and societal possessions.

In the 8th house, we strive to acquire a function, a position, that gives us status and prestige. We become managers of estates or civil servants who represent laws of the land; we identify with the powers of state.

With difficult positions in the 8th house, we tend to behave conformistically. We hide behind orders from above or behind what others demonstrate as models and pillars of society. We receive the means of others, become successors to greater minds, walk in the footsteps of others or take over dynastic mandates.

The conformative behavior can reach such a state that we do not live for ourselves but live through others. We can lose contact to real life by playing out roles and functions. Only the outer facade, the machinery, works, never questioning the reason of life and its relationship to others. We can become a misanthrope and lose contact with the most inner being. Psychological and spiritual crises can develop, contained in the "die and rise again" process descriptive of this Scorpio house.

These crises begin when form, structure, and laws (with their mechanical application) have taken over or when a condition in effect for a long time begins to be broken up from the outside. Suppressed life expression, the "I" that has been captured in mechanical routinization with a thousand handcuffs of responsibility, revolts and wants to be free. Then we ask: what sense is there in this, why try so hard, should we put up indefinitely with rules and laws, responsibilities and problems? A gnawing doubt awakens.

Depending upon which planets are positioned in the 8th house (especially with Saturn), this doubt will be constantly in the forefront of life. Out of this can develop the "wisdom of the pessimist", renouncing all initially in order to escape pain. We feel unable to do anything against existing conditions, and we think: "there is no sense to it all". With certain tensions especially, when we do not get what we want, we give up and sink into despair and self-pity.

With difficult astrological contacts, self-destructive tendencies can develop, or we accuse others, society, god and the world, blaming them for our own shortcomings.

The 8th house is a difficult area; we must be careful not to lose ourselves because of societal responsibilities and the inner urge to play a role in society. It is not an accident that this house is called the "death house" in old astrology.

The Axis Cross in the House System

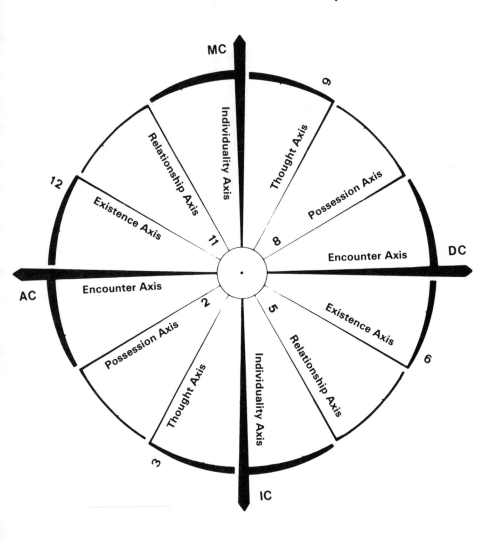

Cardinal	House 1 / 7	I-YOU Axis, Encounter
	House 4 /10	Individuality Axis
Fixed	House 2 / 8	Possession Axis
	House 5 / 11	Relationship Axis
Mutable	House 3 / 9	Thought Axis
	House 6 /12	Existence Axis

The Polarity of the Axes

The opposite poles in dualistic analysis and the possible balance of tensions through the "third pole".

We find where the individual meets his environment and the people within it in one of the houses of our astrological system. The zodiac with its signs shows us of what that individual is comprised and what he can become. The house system indicates his station, his spheres of interests, the life arenas in whch he acts and reacts.

We are placed into our environment, are dependent upon it, and therein experience ourselves. We and our environment: that is the practical life. That is why the house system is the most immediate and interesting part of modern astrology. This is where confrontatons occur between the "I" and the YOU, the individual and the collective. Here we find social tensions and also opportunities for balance in all spheres of human relationships.

But just as the problems in inter-human spheres can not be solved on the basis of either-or, good or bad, the traditional dualistic way of viewing the house system and its axis polarities is not the best approach.

If there is an approach at all, then it can only be found in a *third* possibility, the "third pole".

To understand easier this concept of a "third pole", let us examine the house system and its axis polarities more closely.

THE POLAR OPPOSITES IN THE FIXED CROSS

The Fixed Axis: 2/8   Possession Axis

Let us examine first the 2/8 axis purely dualistically, by emphasizing the contrasts of the poles. We will see that the contrasts that are inherent in the cusps of the 2nd and 8th houses are incompatible. The problems growing out of these opposites are only soluable when we free ourselves from a concept of dualistic analysis.

When we call the 2/8 polarity the possession axis, this is so far correct since both houses have something to do with this general reference, yet, in a very different sense. We see that the 2nd house is normally called the "money house" and the 8th house is called the "death house". With such general terms we can hardly be specific about the polar connection of these two houses. However, we start with the zonal placement of these two houses, then we can begin to recognize the connection. The 2nd house is on the left side, in the "I"-hemisphere of the horoscope. It represents *MY* possessions. The 8th house is on the right side, in the YOU-hemisphere. It represents *YOUR* possessions. So it becomes clear why, in the literature, the 8th house is also called the house of "inheritance".

We equate possessions with substances from which we draw energy, we find an explanation for the fact that the possession axis houses also have to do with food. People with accentuated 2nd and 8th houses tend, as a rule, to voluminous meals for the purpose of gaining sufficient substance. We can also equate substance with provisions. A tendency toward provisions is a typical characteristic of the 2nd house. We stockpile our supplies in siloes and secure them well so that nobody can get near our possessions: what I own, nobody can take from me. And the extreme form of securing possessions is greed.

My strong instinct for possessions can also apply to the possessions of others, the possessions shown in the 8th house. Possibly the possessions there are greater than my own. If I am a decent human being, then I will wait until I get my hands on these possessions legally, which means I wait until the other is dead in order to inherit them. But if I am an asocial human being, then I will want to get them now, with violence if necessary.

So, it is inheritance and death in the 8th house; death also for *me* if I use violence and the lawful punishment affects me.

Of course, I can relinquish the possessions of the 8th house or I *must* renounce them, must watch how others live in plenty. What is left for me then is envy. Greed in the 2nd house, envy in the 8th house; two all too human weaknesses within this polarity, this possession axis!

Envy can kill the human being: death in the 8th house.

We have created laws to protect our possessions against unlawful takeovers. laws are restrictions, barriers within which we are kept; laws force us into some form of renunciation. We suffer under this renunciation. So there is pain in this possession angle that is unexplainable or, in its causes is difficult to recognize.

My possessions, your possessions. The wish for more possessions, also for that of others. The law protects my possessions but also keeps me within barriers.

Wish here, renunciation there, and ensuing pain.

It is the axis where, in earlier days, the law "an eye for an eye and a tooth for a tooth" belonged. In the 2nd house, one's own possessions were thought of as untouchable; in the 8th house, the possessions of the clan. Woe be it if someone touched those possessions; often the guilt was only assuaged by death (blood revenge).

This blood revenge, its taboos and protective laws were all related to the 2/8 axis and also to the 5/11 axis, because the wife was also a possession, and if she was desired by someone else, then this act could only be avenged through death. Also, we had duels, officers' honor, honor codes. These are the polar contrasts of the possession axis: two astrologically related houses that show polarity conflict clearly. The solution to the conflict lies beyond the either-or of the 2/8 axis, as we shall see later.

The Fixed Axis: 5/11   *Relationship Axis*

We must distinguish here again left and right house-orientation. Naturally, it does not mean that the position of the 11th house in the "I"-hemisphere excludes the relations to the YOU, but rather that the accentuation is on the "I". With the 5th house, the accentuation is on the YOU.

Actually, the behavior forms are accordingly quite different in these two houses.

In the 5th house we pursue the other person. We attack him; aggressive contacts can develop. Typically, in the act of making contact in the 5th house, we have our own "system", always the same trick or artful technique with which to be successful with the YOU.

The contact in the 5th house is definitely instinctive; we seek a physical relationship to the sexual YOU.

That everyone works here with his special tactic, his tricks or impress-behavior has decisive significance in the choice of partners, because not everybody "falls for" one's tactics! With my style, I will only attract a certain number of possible partners. I strike a chord only in people who complement my being through my basic mechanism of making contacts with others. Each person seeks in the partner the ideal complement. Naturally, one hundred percent complement would be ideal. If that complement is only about 50 per cent, then the human being will seek out the other missing 50 per cent, which means he or she will look for it in several partners, while in the case of a marriage only one can be legal.

The "illegal" ones are the cause for marital drama. Of course, for moral reasons, I can renounce the missing percentage. Then I will suffer, and the pain can lead to tragic events. Often, a marriage suffers from a low complementation percentage; unfulfilled needs accumulate, and the end result is aggression.

The 5th house therefore offers several possibilities for smaller and bigger dramas that have their real causes, similar to the other fixed axis, in the *wish to possess*. Here, I want to possess the other person all for myself. I become afraid when the other's gaze wanders; my jealousy awakens. If the wish to possess the other person takes on extreme forms, we find enslavement.

If I find that my wish to possess the other individual is not fulfilled, I will resign after much effort; then my wish to possess becomes political. I seek power over the collective. Now I do not want this form of power to possess, but rather *to control* (which is an indirect form of possession). One who does not find fulfillment in a "love trip" seeks the "power trip"!

In the 5th house, we seek direct contact to the YOU. Here we find ourselves in the midst of colorful, human happenings, and we give our instincts (even if predictable) free rein. Not so in the opposite 11th house in the "I"-hemisphere. Here we look from lofty heights, from an air-house, from a distance onto the frolicking happenings. At the very same time, we are aware of the loss of fun. In the 11th house, we are far away from the daily bustle; we become philosophers who tend toward observation of the self and toward critical evaluation of others. In the 11th house we find a way back to ourselves.

As in all fixed houses, the 11th house also collects something. Here, what we collect are realizations that we have gained from knowing others. Here human ideals are created. At the same time, we can recognize our own ideas in the 11th house. In all cases, when there is a strong accentuation of the 11th house, we find not only a strongly formed conception of man, but we also make quite high demands upon his social behavior. In the extreme case, crusades will be led, fire and sword used; masses can become so fanatisized that there is no doubt left about the final victory.

The love/power trip of the 5th house and the human ideals and their defense in the 11th house are poles that, in a dualistic analysis, again exist in an either-or situation, as we have already seen in study of the 2/8 axis.

We first observed polar contrasts in the *fixed* cross of the house system because fixity is more easily observable than cardinality and mutability. We will also study the contrasts and incompatibility of dualistic analysis on the cardinal and mutable crosses, but, for the moment, it is important to establish most clearly the limitation of either-or thinking. We strongly need a third dimension, a "third pole" to free ourselves from the tensions of contrasts.

THE SOLUTIONS, THE WAY OUT OVER THE "THIRD POLE"

The Fixed Cross example

Since the chapter about the incompatibility of the axis polarity in the fixed cross is still fresh in our memory, we will use it to demonstrate how to become free from polar tensions and dualisitc analysis. In the next chapter, we will examine the same problems and their solutions on the cardinal and mutable crosses.

It is in the nature of the fixed houses that conditions can not be abruptly changed. Changes come only in small steps and with much expenditure of energy. The fixed cross is anchored. With oppositions on these axes, especially, so very much can be said; so very many "tales to be told".

How can we find a solution, a liberation from axis polarity? We need a third dimension. For example: if tension exists in the 2/8 axis, in the possession axis, then we will find the solution in the second fixed axis, houses 5/11, the relationship axis. (Huber's concept of relationship is 5/11; to 1/7 he gives the sense of encounter. Review the drawing on page 80.

Those who live through an opposition in the tension area of the possession axis, are one-sidedly oriented toward the practical-technical. They see only the mechanics, how they work like a computer, and they seek in this fashion to solve possession problems—even with force, if not possible otherwise. They believe themselves to be able to organize everything.

Whoever is so deeply caught up in the problems of possessions of the 2/8 axis can only be helped by the dimension of the 5/11 axis: the human dimension. He must turn away from "things", from substance, *toward human beings*, then he will find freedom from this ensnarement. He must move away from the possession axis toward the relationship axis, but not one sidedly to *one* pole of the other axis; rather, toward the other *axis as a whole.*

We free ourselves from the tension field of the possession poles of the 2/8 axis by consciously seeking the human dimension as it is contained in the 5/11 axis. This other axis crosses the first axis. It is seen not as another polarity but as a dynamic unit. This is the "third pole" that offers us true solutions. The solution will always be found on that axis of the cross that is occupied by fewer or no tension factors. I repeat, it is important that we see this "solution axis" as a unit and not - as with dualistic analysis - another contrast of axial poles. Let us be clearly conscious of this: we are seeking in the other axis a less tense, less problematic unit of expression. We see then, for example, on the poles of the 5/11 axis, *not* the contrast of eroticism and human idealism but, rather, we understand the axis as an opportunity for the expansion of human thinking and feeling.

We have not only the contrast but the *synthesis* of the axis poles. We only have to think about it: the spiritual ideal of man in the 11th house and the animalistic instinctive side of the 5th house are arenas for myriad combination possibilities of positive inter-human relationships.

The difficulties between two people when viewed this way, for example in a marriage, result from a fixation upon one tension axis. If the tensions are in the inter-human sphere, the 5/11 axis, then we must look for balance, for a way out thrugh the 2/8 axis. We will find one if we take advantage of the opportunity offered by a matter-of-fact approach to the difficulty. Both eroticism and economy must be workable in a marriage. Tensions in the erotic area often have their roots in the neglect of the economic area. The same holds true the other way around. Sex and money are often connected. If we are aware of our possibilities to alleviate tensions with the other axis of the grand cross, then we have a much easier time with the problems.

THE POLAR OPPOSITES IN THE CARDINAL CROSS

The Cardinal Axis 4/10	*Individuality Axis*
The Cardinal Axis 1/7	*Encounter Axis*

We have talked about this axis in detail in the chapter about the collective and individuality spheres and the "I" and YOU hemispheres. We will concentrate now only on the polar opposites and their possible solutions.

The 1/7 axis from the AC to the DC is the *encounter axis*. The difference between this axis and the relationship axis 5/11 is mainly that here we have processes of dynamic activity and action while in the relationship axis it is the *format* of the relationship that is more important.

On the 1/7 axis, the "I' and YOU meet for mutual comparison. We search critically for the weaknesses and strengths of the YOU, and we make plus or minus evaluations. The axis 1/7 is the arena of competition, of comparison in all areas of life, from sport contests to courtship. The "I" wants to outdo the YOU, to impress him, at least to be on the same level. Here we find the fight for existence in its most severe forms, but here also take place the encounters arranged by love.

These are the extremes of this axis.

Persons with strong left accentuation of this axis, especially with Sun and Moon positions strongly "I"-accentuated are egoistical or ego-centric.

If the accentuation is on the DC, in the 7th house then the experience of harmony is sought out. This can go so far as to lose the "I", a self-estrangement can occur, and life is lived only for the YOU. Egoism and altruism are the tension poles to be mastered.

On the 4/10 axis, tensions arise from the connection of the IC and MC, from the contrast between the collective (4th house) and the individual (10th house). The person born into a collective tries very early to become an individual and rise above the masses.

This effort can be quickly recognized when the 10th house is strongly occupied. Then we normally find a strongly defined individualist.

The tensions of this axis will be seriously activated when the collective expels the individual or when the individual ignores the collective. The collective demands a uniform behavior of its members. This uniform collective behavior is exactly what the individual feels as a hindrance and as something to be overcome. He must behave differently than the members of the collective and this puts him into grave opposition to them.

On the other hand, in his own interest, man can not completely dispense with the collective; he would be without defense. The collective protects its members, but for the price of the collective behavior itself. And there is where the difficulties begin for the individualist. Does he even have an alternative?

THE SOLUTION OF THE AXIS POLARITY 4/10

The solution lies, as with the fixed cross, in the "third pole", that is, in the other axis of the cross. The solution is in the encounter. The individualist may do more than confront his collective; he may stay above it, but he should not look down on it. Even as an individualist, he must remain a human being and see in others the same human dimension, equal to him in a biological sense. He must not lose the real human contact with the YOU; he should always seek and maintain it. Active encounter, the 1/7 axis, is the "third pole", the way out of the polarity axis 4/10.

THE SOLUTION OF THE AXIS POLARITY 1/7

The problem of the I-YOU 1/7 axis is to strive for individual development, which means we should become free from YOU-dependency and develop into independent personalities.

Those who are too dependent upon the YOU and cannot live without it will experience disappointment over and over again. We always worry that we are not accepted by the YOU, that we are wrongly evaluated. We are afraid of disregard, degradation and rejection. We always strive to secure the affection and support of the YOU. We are ready with all kinds of manipulative techniques and a net of defense mechanisms for any situation - against attacks or just reactions from the YOU - to react with deliberation or diplomatic strategy.

In this way, each real and living contact, each natural exchange between the "I" and YOU is made more difficult, if not impossible.

The resulting contact difficulties and dependency with the YOU that exist through tensions (opposition) on the encounter axis (AC/DC) can only be solved when we switch to the other polar axis 4/10 and become aware of the self on the individuality axis. That is where we will straighten to our full height; with an elevated head we gain a wider overview and, at the same time, a backbone with which we stand steadily. We recognize how wrongly we confronted the YOU and how we can make it better. We determine seriously to change and cultivate a new attitude toward the YOU. We evaluate the YOU correctly and see other people as they really are. Free of wish projection and hallucination we can encounter the YOU; a real exchange becomes possible through which we ourselves and the YOU become happier. Only when we are strengthened within and when we can live and exist on our own are we able to be a real partner to the YOU.

THE POLAR OPPOSITES IN THE MUTABLE CROSS: AXES 12/6 and 3/9

In the cross of the mutable houses, the polarity is not so strongly pronounced as in the cardinal or fixed cross (where it is the most painful). It can happen that the contrast of the poles in the mutable cross are barely noticeable, which can be explained through the adjustable characteristics of these houses.

The Changeable Axis 12/6   *Existence Axis*

On the left side, in the 12th house, the question about existence is asked on its own terms, the question about one's own existence is put into consciousness. Here we think and meditate quietly about our "I". Meditation and contemplation belong to the core of this house that is placed in the "I"-hemisphere. The environment is at a distance.

On the right side, in the 6th house, we are confronted with the YOU. The question of existence is concretely asked at work and in cooperation with the YOU. This cooperation will only work if we are objectively, realistically, and humanly prepared. We can fail here in every respect. That is the problem of this house. If I recognize that there are difficulties mainly in the human area, then I best retreat into the stillness of the 12th house. In the 12th house, I can recognize and experience myself as I really am. By going within myself, I come nearer to my own core substance. Equipped with the self-confidence that I find there, I will appear again, more successfully, on the outside and will win the fight for existence.

If I am not successful in the securing of the self, then the world and its demands become a burden. I feel crushed by responsibilities and work; I am unable to master them; I give up. Most often, it is lacking self-confidence that will let me fail with work in the 6th house.

The existence axis 6/12 has to do with self-confidence in a direct sense. Not the external self-confidence that is shown everywhere, but the inner conviction that "I am", that I am here for a purpose and that I am needed. This is connected with the existential basic question of life, with the right for existence and finally with "being". This question is felt on the axis over and over again within the realities of life. It is existence in the sense of "to be or not to be" that is the problem here and that can only be solved from our spiritual or inner-psychological side.

In the 12th house, I must be honest with myself and recognize where I stand, what I am, what strengths and weaknesses I have. The question is, do I have something to give to the world, am I of use, am I able to fulfill my tasks? Why do I fail in life and with my work? Am I a burden to others? Am I able to exist by myself?

The 6th house is the real arena of the fight for existence. It is an acute area; we must do something. Not only is the activity important, but also the HOW of the activity. We watch ourselves and the environment. How are things done? What is being expected? What must we be able to do, to bring with us, in order to hold our own with others? It is important to find out where we can function optimally through our abilities, where the right place is for us, where our talents are needed. Finding this out in the 6th house becomes the best proof of our self-confidence and of our successful fight for existence. Self-confidence is being built by our own capacity for achievement and work.

Through friction, disagreement, failure, defeat at work and in life, we become painfully conscious of our shortcomings and faults. We try with all we have to overcome these faults, to educate ourselves further, to broaden our knowledge, to improve ourselves and reach an accordingly better position. In a positive expression, we will try everything to appear as competent as possible at our work place and to mean something special to fellow workers and bosses through good work and a warm and social behavior. This can be overdone, and we can appear subservient, fawning, and servile. Self-awareness is gone; we let others walk over us, we are exploited, often because we are afraid to lose our position, our job.

In the 6th house, much work is done; we overexert easily, we take on burdens and work that are often unnecessary and are beyond our strength. With certain planetary positions, we even insist on being allowed to carry the load for the YOU because we then feel heroic and effective. We build our self-confidence on the grounds of being of service and use to others.

Tensions on the Existence axis often point to a conflict between the demands of life and the possibilities and abilities to comply. Often it is the fear of possible failure, of personal defeat or rejection that makes it impossible to find one's place in life. We almost flee into the 12th house and hide from others, we become reserved, shy, suspicious; we build an illusionary world which has nothing to do with reality. This conflict of the mastery of existence or the failure of the outer life is often the cause behind self-delusion through drug-trips, leaving reality and fleeing into fantasy and dreams.

But the problems are not solved this way, and over and over again we must face the reality of life and find out through the 6th house how we can find the way to earn our living and support ourselves. When we are not successful and do not get what we try to achieve, then it is only a small step to compensate for defeat by becoming ill or behaving dysfunctionally.

Failure at work, in the earning of an existence, almost always leads to some form of illness. It can be temporary because everybody, sometime in life, suffers a defeat; it can also become chronic. Most often, psychosomatic processes cause illness, and these processes are indicated on the existence axis. In every horoscope in the positions of the 6th house or the opposite tensions of the 6/12 axis, we can see how we react to the psychosomatic mechanism when failure or pressure is put upon it. Often the process of becoming ill is a natural defense mechanism of nature. We do not always quit on our own. In our modern achievement oriented society, we want to keep going. We believe that "without us it won't work" or "I have no time to relax", until finally nature asks its due and we become ill.

There are many forms of correct or incorrect behavior on this axis. One form not mentioned yet is the asocial or criminal behavior. If someone for example does not wish to work and sees the solution to his problems as living at the expense of the YOU, to use his intelligence and charm to subdue other people to serve him and care for him, then someday this will turn on itself. Such encroachments will be rejected by the YOU and the environment, and, with criminal acts, the law will intervene. Such people are isolated and put into prison; which is the 12th house.

The 12th house is the house of chosen or forced isolation. If we are sick, we are in the 12th house, be that at home in our own bedroom alone or in the hospital. If we did something wrong or earned our existence under false pretenses, then others will isolate us. We have humanly failed when we have damaged the YOU and not recognized his rights. What does not work out in the 6th house reacts in the 12th. One brings out the other; the polarities hang together, are causally connected.

THE SOLUTION OF THE AXIS POLARITY 6/12

Here also the "third pole" offers help through the second axis in this mutable cross, the thinking axis 3/9. Those who have existence problems on the 6/12 axis should try to think philosophically about life. Through recognition, we gain insight and arrive at the correct behavior for the inter-human arena.

In the 3rd house, we can gain a good education and prepare for life. We observe how others do it and gather a wealth of information from the collective . . . all that we are missing and is helpful for study and work advancement.

In the 9th house, we recognize that there are also other concerns. We expand our consciousness, free ourselves from the small or big worries of existence and win a clear overview. Things take on a meaningful order in relation to each other. It feels good to look up, to breathe freely in a spiritual atmosphere free of routine problems. From this raised viewpoint, we can see in a corrected perspective things that have burdened us. We can take a direction free of existence pressures and find new meaning.

The Mutable Axis 3/9   Thinking Axis

When observing this axis, we must remember that the 3rd house is in the collective sphere and the 9th house is in the individual sphere. *In the 3rd house*, the collective provides the thought models: the accepted knowledge of the collective is offered to us in the family and in school, from sisters, brothers and teachers.

Soon the individual develops his own critical faculties and finds that the practical experience and the knowledge within the collective is not necessarily the ultimate truth.

He observes, gains his own opinion about things, has his own thoughts and creates the basis for his own life philosophy which is placed in the 9th house.

Two types confont each other on this axis: first the type who accepts the stereotyped thinking of the collective without question and then the thinking person who suffers loneliness because of his individual philosophy and - in contrast to the collective thinker - is plagued with scruples.

The 9th house in the individuality sphere brings out, in contrast to the collective way of thinking, the process of individual self-becoming. First, we find ourselves in confrontation with what is popular opinion; we meet conflict because we fight existing opinion. For our own convictions, we often have to accept the misunderstanding of our closest relatives in the 3rd house and separate ourselves from standardized behavior, from normal values in order to reach an inner independence in our way of thinking. Then we find the necessary courage to defend our convictions and develop individualized thinking and behavior.

In the 3rd house, it is not so simple to free oneself from collective thought habits. We think in terms of certain structures and models and we are often unaware that these are part of a social situation adopted automatically to steer our subconscious thinking.

Certain thought formations are sometimes difficult for us because they do not correspond to established norms. When new thought structures are put before us, they often appear to us to be strange, devious and "heretical". It can happen that we fight against them and reject them as bad and false. Sometimes, simply a moral verdict is pronounced. We believe that the case is finished, and we do not have to make any more effort. We have our peace and we can continue in the old way. There are people who stay in their circle of thoughts and defend at all cost what has always had validity, what has always been done and thought in a certain way. They categorically reject anything new; they rail against "those 9th house people" who always come up with new ideas and disturb the peace. This is an important problem of the 3/9 axis.

In the 9th house it is otherwise. There are always original thought processes under way that are not based on the old routined thought habits. They lead to individual results through intensive reflection. In the 9th house, we know that we can think for ourselves and we are convinced that we know things as well or even better than others. In the 3rd house, we believe that others know everything, our teachers and professors, the minister, priest or rabbi, the parents. We do not have an individual opinion, and we are afraid to say what we think. It is always assumed that the others are right, and whether something is correct or incorrect is not considered.

The individual clearly has these two possibilities: in his thinking, he can remain "in line", bound to the collective, and continue along within the models and structures that have been presented to him, or he can have the courage to be suspicious of them and begin slowly to free himself from them all, developing upward toward the 9th house, from the "near 3rd house" to the "distant 9th house". This means that we are willing to be impressed by things beyond our own horizon, to accept them as truth and reality, to try to understand them. In this way, an expansion of consciousness and real growth are possible. The attraction to seek out new thought directions is in the 9th house.

Depending upon the positions in the 3rd and 9th houses, we can see if an individual is conservative and sticks to the old or if he is seeking new directions and is mentally able to absorb and learn more.

There is also the extreme type in the 9th house who *always* comes up with new thoughts and ideas, who accepts nothing prevailing and questions everything that has been established through tradition and culture. His desire to be especially original, to think differently than all others can lead to a mania. He gets lost in theories that are not practicably applicable but which he presents to all with great conviction. When others show no understanding, he punishes them with contempt and views their mediocrity as collective-bound, conforming to "good citizenship". He is difficult for many others because he only speaks of himself and his own ideas, perceives of himself as better than others, is always right, and is not interested in anything else but his own thoughts.

THE SOLUTION OF THE AXIS POLARITY 3/9

Here again, we come to the "third pole" that offers the solution. The necessity to support his own existence urges the theoretician of the *9th house* to become "normal"; to come down to earth and work like everyone else. Even the intellectual presumptiveness often found with independent thinkers can be balanced through the existence axis. On the 6/12 axis we are confronted with the reality of life, with the trials for survival not only of ourselves but of others. The recognition of how many suffering people there are in the world can touch the intellectually arrogant and awake the wish to help, heal and serve seen in the 6/12 axis. He becomes humble, learning to feel a responsibility toward the suffering masses within his independent overview. He will concentrate his thought energies toward a solution to the many problems of human existence and be active by teaching, advising and healing.

The 3rd house person does not get along very well any more with his outdated thought habits. In the fight for existence, it turns out that those habits are not useful anymore; he must make an effort to adjust his way of thinking to the new and present time. He notices by his failures that he can not continue in the same way, that he must change. He will think about it until he has an idea, finds a way out of his dilemma.

On the realistic 6/12 existence axis, the 3/9 axis contrasts meet. In the practical application of the mastery of life, it shows that collective thinking as well as individual thinking must prove themselves in life. Even the individualist will recognize that there are many valuable sides to collective thinking that cannot be simply thrown overboard. There is a middle ground: the grooved and habitual thought habits and results that prove valuable and correct and can be checked against reality will be kept in use. Where thought habits, prejudices, fixed opinions and attitudes collide with reality again and again, new explanations and better ways must be sought out; or at least, we must seek them out openly.

SUMMARY

The two axes of the mutable cross always have to do with recognition. In the 12th house, it is the recognition of the inner being and the reason for existence: am I or am I not? In the 6th house, it is the recognition of the world and my relationship to this world in the sense of existence, how can I find my place, my place in the market? In the 3rd house, it is the recognition of the origin and structure of thoughts, what we bring with us for the beginning of our own "thinking career" in life. And in the 9th house, the end results of this thinking and recognition of all mutable houses are expressed in our own self-wrought life philosophy.

Each man has a philosophy with which he explains his life. This philosophy is to be found in the 9th house. The questions about the reason for life surface there. The questions for the reasons of life in the 9th house show up the connection with the existence axis. In the 9th house, the important focus is basic recognition that does not necessarily involve existence survival, but feeds on a special recognition situation, on the ability or inability to tackle life and to give it meaning.

We have tried with examples of all three axis crosses to show the problems of those people who see the contrasts of the pole axes exclusively dualistically. We have recognized how solutions and exits were offered over the "third pole", the second axis of the same cross. We keep a third avenue open between good and bad, either/or, to lead us out of a dilemma.

The Intensity Curve

We come to a chapter that is very important for the differentiated judgement of planets in the house system. It is the intensity-curve or line that indicates a three part differentiation in the sphere of activity of each house.

For a closer look, see the drawing below.

Around the outer circle runs a carefully graduated curved line that we call the *intensity curve*. This line has a wave-like motion through the whole house system and reaches its highest intensity at each house cusp. It then descends to the so-called "zero-point" or "low-point" of house intensity. This point in reality corresponds to the "golden mean" of the house.*

This intensity curve, corresponding to house cusps and the golden mean, indicates that the strongest and weakest points of a house are already beginning at the "low-point" of the preceeding house, that they are strongest at the cusp and extend to the "low-point" of the next house. This corroborates that different areas of life overlap.

As already mentioned earlier, the house does not begin at the house cusp and does not abruptly end at the next cusp. The qualities of the houses intermingle and penetrate each other to a certain degree, resulting in a coloring of areas of interest and allowing an even finer differentiation. *With this curve and our special areas, we can instantly recognize and specify the intensity and effectiveness of a planet, of a force.*

But first let us pay attention briefly to the measurement of the golden mean.

THE GOLDEN MEAN

In dynamic space analysis, the law of the "golden mean" has important meaning. As we know, the golden mean is a division of distance. The smaller portion of which is in relationship to the bigger portion as the bigger portion is to the whole distance.

$$\frac{a}{b} = \frac{b}{(a+b)}$$ approximately 3:5 (exactly: $1 = 0.382 + 0.618$)

The golden mean can be determined from both points of a line. Here is a geometrical example:

THE PENTAGRAM

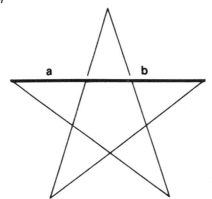

---

* This point was found after long examination and only afterwards was recognized as the golden mean. That is why there is a small discrepancy in the third decimal of the golden mean (0.615 instead of 0.618).

The pentagram comes into being because five points within a circle in equal distance to each other are connected with lines (5x72°) but always one is passed over. Each line is crossed by two others. The resulting line division relationship is always in the measure of the golden mean.

We find the same laws in the human body. In earlier days the human being was drawn within the pentagram, with the five centers (head, hands, feet) in the respective corners. This harmonious relationship of measurement is also shown in leaf structures and in many other forms of nature as well as in the art and architecture of antiquity and the renaissance.

The application of the golden mean in the horoscope shows an even flow of natural laws, with the continuous curve line going through the horoscope (easily seen in the drawing on page 94). The cusp points indicate the most vital, pulsating forces of the houses; in the wave thoughts, the so-called "low-points", the energies are still and are gathered and processed and matured for a new ascent.

We can compare this energy play with centrifugal and centripetal force. At the cusps of the houses, the energies push outwards (centrifugal) and at the "low-points" they collapse within (centripetal). There, they are attracted toward their own center, receive new energy, direction and goals in order to be flung out again. This rhythm takes place in accordance with the golden mean.

The golden mean measurement can be applied to the house wheel in one or the other direction. In *clockwise* motion, we find our so-called "invert-point" of each house; in *counter-clockwise* motion, the "low-point".

Let us stay for a moment with the centrifugal force example and imagine that we have a stone on a string, swinging it in a circle: the right turn corresponds to the "invert-point" and the left turn to the "low-point". Psychologically, left is always inside, right outside. We can also picture these forces as spirals: the spirals toward the inside turn to the left, the spirals toward the outside turn to the right ("6" and "9").

THE INTENSITY DIFFERENCE OF HOUSES AND SIGNS

The law of the golden mean measured in the intensity curve *is repeated in sign qualities*. The signs are the energy sources of the planets, and it was always thought that the signs were strongest approximately in their middle. Close to the sign borders, the energy manifestation is obviously relatively weak.

If we apply this golden mean measurement to the signs, by "turning right" around the zodiac, we discover the 12th degree in each sign. If a planet is positioned in the 12th degree of a sign, it has the greatest energy; it receives from the sign a greater potential of energy than if it were at the beginning or end of a sign.

The sign system points to the inclination already there at birth. If we analyse a planet in a sign, we get information about where influential energies come from, about the hereditary and constitutional factors that determine planetary influence.

If we look at a planet within a house, it becomes clear into which direction the specific inclinations go in practical life, in which areas of life they express themselves. That is why the house system is a centrally important point in psychological horoscope analysis.

We want to look in greater detail at three important points: the house cusp, the "invert-point", and the "low-point", separately and interrelatedly.

THE HOUSE CUSPS

Quality: The house cusps are zones of high activity. Energies accumulate most strongly here and are intensely directed externally.

At the cusps, productivity potency and vitality are realized. There is an impetus that starts energies moving. The energies indicated by the planet can be used fully in life. Externalization in life reaches its highest peak. We overlook borders and can also easily go too far.

All planetary energies on house cusps flow outward, are always ready to be applied to the environment, are noticed from the outside and bring immediate results. It can happen that, for quite some time, we perceive in a person only the cusp-accentuated planets and then, after getting to know the person better, we discover *other* characteristics that have been hidden in the inner areas or at the "low-point".

Concept: All the qualities of planets that are on or near a housecusp can be fully and effectively used in life. These planets react strongly to outside stimulation and gain fulfillment through the environment.

Operation:

Of course, a planet is not always directly on a cusp; it can be before or after the cusp. These zones before and after also have special concepts.

Psychologically viewed, behavior reaching for a peak can bring about specific "crisis mechanisms". *Before* the peak or cusps of a house, we must exert much to reach the goal. This exertion can become *too* much, so that it can collapse before fulfillment. We would like to give up, to slump, and to resign. Depending on our natures, this situation can also inspire us to extraordinary performances (compensation). The danger of the cusp is that the energies are not under control and that we begin projects full of enthusiasm and senselessly waste energies in the euphoria of reaching fulfillment.

After the cusp, the curve goes down again introducing a different psychological attitude: the "high" is weakened; the new vista and vision we worked so hard for *before the peak-cusp* can now be transformed into reality. This occurs after the cusp point almost naturally and without toil, and we can enjoy the fruits of previous exertions.

Example:

This effect may be seen in the following example. We know that each house has a psychological theme, a definite sphere of intersts and activities.

The 9th house is concerned with a personally constructive and productive way of thinking, with philosophy, mental and spiritual attitudes. All planets in the 9th house are concerned with these themes, but there are differences that result from *where* the planet is positioned in the house. A planet before the cusp of the 9th house is already interested in philosophy. Although that planet is still in the 8th house and still occupied with societal concerns and responsibilities, it already begins to be interested in the freedom of creative thinking, starting from the lowest point in the outer intensity line, *from the "low-point" of the 8th house onward.*

When a planet is found before the 10th cusp, the person is still philosophizing (according to the quality of the planet), but he is already interested in this career; he wants to realize what he has thought about!

Planets before a house cusp are at a crossroads; they are still occupied with the theme of their house but, at the same time, strive with their interests toward the next house. The energies develop concentration within the coming theme.

Planets after the cusp identify themselves fully and definitely with the theme of that house. Because of this focused identity, they are successful in life. Therefore, generally, they are more effective than planets before a house cusp.

This is an important differentiation, especially in the analysis of the horoscope of twins, when often the only, but very important, difference is that one twin's planet will be before a cusp and the other twin's same planet will be after the cusp. Generally speaking, the area between the beginning of a house and the "low-point" are the most intensive, the most effective, because the house theme is in highest focus. And, in this area, there is still another reference point that deserves attention.

THE "INVERT-POINT"

The golden mean in each house measured clockwise.

The "low-point" is at the lowest point of the intensity curve, and the "invert-point" is mirrorlike next to it. We normally measure the "low-point" distance from a house cusp *forward*; now we will measure it from the next house cusp *backward*.

Quality: *The "invert-point" points to a gathering of energy that originates through the fall of energy from the house cusp to the energy-stop at the "low-point". Psychologically, this dwindling of energy forces a heightened concentration of the remaining energies onto goals that can be realized and have long-term effect.*

On the house cusps, the planets or corresponding behavioral functions are, outwardly, intensely effective. They often are so expansive that they are difficult to control and can easily lead to an energy depletion. If the planets are past the strong stimulation of the cusp point, they move toward the braking, halting area of the "low-point" and require a resourcefully stronger concentration of energy. On the one hand, there is still an energy push from the house cusp; on the other, already enough braking influence which demands an especially disciplined handling of the available energies and abilities indicated by the planets in this section of the house.

Concept: *All characteristics of planets standing at the "invert-point" or nearby can be consciously controlled and intelligently focused, made productive in life. They react to the person's will.*

Operation:

At the "invert-point" the intensity curve reaches a certain low point. We become aware that energies are not limitless, that we must use them carefully and thoughtfully in order not to squander them.

At the "invert-point" we reach a point of balance, maintained by will and understanding. But it is not a static point; it's a dynamic balance among cusp, "low", and "invert-points". The relationship among these points is accomplished in an antagonistic balancing process. Each force controls others. Through this disciplinary action, the planets at the "invert-point" can be used successfully and focused in life. Impulse does not override goal, and the stabilizing forces do not lead into over-crystallized or solidified condition. Things, projects, or plans that are begun at the "invert-point" do have stability and are of long duration because they are viable. In this sense, we can also call this point the "living point".

The idea, the vision, the impulse can be brought in accord with reality; the correct viable form is found and created to express plans and wishes. This is a true creative process, accomplished with intelligence and awarely directed will. One's own creative energies can be realized productively and successfully. Self-confidence strengthens success in great measure because we can realize ourselves within this position. It is helpful, with possible weak areas of self confidence, to use the planets or functioning organs positioned at the "invert-points" for particular strengthening of the self.

Example:

When the Sun is placed at the "invert-point", then the person has special self-awareness; he knows what he can do and evaluates his abilities correctly. He concentrates on a goal to be reached and avoids all speculative or irresponsible acts. He uses all his energies for one project and is able to make the best of it. Everything superfluous is excluded. The sense of reality is strongly developed and therefore so is the ability to make things happen. (With the Sun at the house *cusp*, in contrast, he tends to overestimate the Self).

But there is also a danger at the "invert-point": the delusion of beginning, doing, concluding everything oneself. One is one's own master, and through one's own will the functioning organs (planets) are controlled and mechaniclly manipulated. A push-button mentality develops. We blockade or activate, open or close, as desired. The necessarily spontaneous reaction of the inner planets especially is severed. Man can become a slave to his own control apparatus if he only applies it for the defense of his own rights or personal interests.

The danger of the "invert-point" then is that we credit success in the world exclusively to personal energies. This creates a wall between the self and others. Loneliness, fear, suspicion, and emptiness often increase at the same rate as we are envied, admired or feared by others. That can lead to inner crises, often reaching the peak at the "low-point".

THE "LOW-POINT"

The golden mean in the houses measured counterclockwise.

When we look at the intensity curve in the drawing on page 94, we can observe that each house also has a low point, where the energy has reached the lowest point.

Quality: At the "low-point" the impulse-giving forces come to rest, to a standstill. Life activity is curbed and is directed toward the inner arena of life. Energies withdraw within. This allows consolidation, deepening, and stabilization. At the "low-point", a maturing process always occurs, a collection inward for new orientation. Here metamorphosis and preparation for new starts take place.

With planets at the "low-points", experiences, all life happenings are analysed, distilled and processed. Depending upon their nature, the planets can lead toward maturation or depressive resignation. At the "low-point", we must "balance the books" and assume the consequences of experience, defeat, failure or unrealized wishes. The "low-point" always has an introspective quality. Here we find entrance to the most inner core being, to our soul areas and our inner life that belong directly to the self. Self-observation and self-awareness are experienced experimentally.

Concept: Qualities indicated by planets at the "low-point" or nearby work on an inner level and can not be fully applied to external life.

Planets positioned at the "low-point" (or closely before or after) will only be effective in the outer world through highest concentration, relentless effort, perserverance, and constancy. There is more there than gets through to the outside. At best, a mature human being who is strengthened within himself, who lives reservedly and introspectively, and who often renounces outside success is called forth.

Operation: In our present performance-oriented times, a "low-point" planet is often critical. There is little interest for our special abilities; there are few overt activities in life. They are not in demand; we can not apply them well. Depending upon the ability, depending upon the planetary influence involved, this can be more or less painful.

The three new planets, the so-called "mental or higher octave planets" Neptune, Uranus, and Pluto, will be less affected than the Sun or Mars, which want to be active and need approval for their activity from the environment. When these energies can not find enough expressive activity outlet in external life, pscyhological and nervous disturbances, depressions and complex emotional frustration can result.

It is important for us to understand the "low-point" positions mainly in their spiritual-cerebral significances. We can view the planetary influences as "entrance points" to the inner core, to the circle in the middle of the horoscope. Then we use the "low-point" positions as opportunities through which we come in contact with the qualities and possibilities of the most inner being. We can consciously direct ourselves toward our own center and discover possibilities for life expression different from the extraverted qualities offered by the house cusps.

Most people do not understand what is being demanded here. They bar development of the inner self at this "low-point". That is why there is much suffering here. We should listen inwardly to observe the will of the central being, to follow the voice, to let go and make room for a new life that wants to be heard. In this way not only will new, fresh energies be freed from the unlimited soul source, but also the roots of the most inner core being will be strengthened. We will live no more through external stimulation and challenges but through and with the inner self. When we have experienced this primal union with the inner core, we seek a basic transformation through new attitudes. We feel the demands for a new stand and a new start.

This turn-around happens at the "low-point"; a letting go of all that has been, all that is habitual and familiar becomes free for renewal. This often signifies a great demand upon the person who cherishes possessions and the joys of achievement. Yet the new becoming depends upon the fulfillment of this inner turn-around. The transformation has to do with the "die and rise again" process that occurs in bigger and smaller dimensions at all "low-points" throughout the houses and which *must* be experienced. Of course, it makes a difference if this "low-point" is in a cardinal, fixed, or mutable house.

In the cardinal houses, the impulse energies are held down at the "low-point" and turned toward the center. This activity can be used as a purpose in itself and can be compensatorily overdone: not producing positive results but leading to desparate depressions or rebellious attempts to break out.

In the fixed houses, the "low-point" introduces a feeling of insecurity and compensates with a rigid perpetuation of prevalent conditions, habits and possessions, leading to a stiff and inflexible condition, often to isolation.

In the mutable houses, the turn-about and acceptance of the new are less difficult. We open our inner self consciously to these new and transforming energies. To strive for new goals is much easier because the preparedness to leave behind static situations is intrinsic to the mutable houses.

In all houses, planets at the "low-points" can suggest sensitive pressure points within self-confidence since, in all cases, external recognition through the environment is quite absent.

Example:

Let us imagine the Sun positioned at the "low-point" of a house, at 12° of a sign (i.e., at the *most intense point in the sign* but the *weakest point in the house*). Self-confidence will have strong potential because it is in the middle of the sign, but it will have no opportunities to find an echo in life since it can not show itself externally.

Most often the environment does not care to know about the self-confidence of such an individual; they walk all over him. The environment says, "You are too egotistical, you must be more humble and not do anything that burdens or upsets others, you will never achieve anything, never produce anything", etc. That's how a "low-point" positioned Sun can manifest (repressive upbringing). The inner potential is strong but the external opportunities are obviously not there. That leads to a blockage of the dynamic life energies. The energies of self-confidence, the urge for self-realization can not flow outwardly; they are held back. This produces depressions, insecurities or the constant feeling of failure. We feel mistaken and, in our most inner self, rejected, misunderstood and lonesome. In some cases, this may lead to over compensatory attempts to break out.

The only possibility for doing something with these "blocked energies" is to turn inward. All energies of these planets, positioned at the "low-point", withdraw within and come in contact with the most inner core energies, as already explained. That's how these so called freeze-point positioned planets or core energies can become springs of spiritual power. We are also compensated this way for the failure to make it as a personality with externally unlimited power.

Our position rule also applies here: if a planet is positioned *before the "low-point"*, then it is strongly under the influence of the forces of persistence and stagnation. The person will resign himself easily and fight the "low-point" experience. He will have difficulties with activating and changing himself. If a planet is *after the "low-point"*, then it has already come into the sphere of influence of the energies holding it back and, through the process of recognition in the changeable zone before the cusp, finds a new way of development. The person accepts "inner values" as measurement standards.

HOUSE SIZE	LOW POINT	HOUSE SIZE	LOW POINT
o	o ′ ″	o	o ′ ″
11	6.45.54	41	25.12.54
12	7.22.48	42	25.49.48
13	7.59.42	43	26.26.42
14	8.36.36	44	27.03.36
15	9.13.30	45	27.40.30
16	9.50.24	46	28.17.24
17	10.27.18	47	28.54.18
18	11.04.12	48	29.31.12
19	11.41.06	49	30.08.06
20	12.18.00	50	30.45.00
21	12.54.54	51	31.21.54
22	13.31.48	52	31.58.48
23	14.08.42	53	32.35.42
24	14.45.36	54	33.12.36
25	15.22.30	55	33.49.30
26	15.59.24	56	34.26.24
27	16.36.18	57	35.03.18
28	17.13.12	58	35.40.12
29	17.50.06	59	36.17.06
30	18.27.00	**60**	36.54.00
31	19.03.54	61	37.30.54
32	19.40.48	62	38.07.48
33	20.17.42	63	38.44.42
34	20.54.36	64	39.21.36
35	21.31.30	65	39.58.30
36	22.08.24	66	40.35.24
37	22.45.18	67	41.12.18
38	23.22.12	68	41.49.12
39	23.59.06	69	42.26.06
40	24.36.00	70	43.03.00
		71	43.39.54
		72	44.16.48

internal gradation

	′ ″
10	6.09
20	12.18
30	18.27
40	24.36
50	30.45

CALCULATING THE "LOW POINTS" IN THE HOUSES

Let us use our example horoscope from page 20. We use a special table for the "low point" calculation (see previous page). In the first column we find the different house sizes that we have to calculate.

1. Example: 1st House

In our example horoscope, the ascendant is 7 Leo and the second house cusp is 1 Virgo. Using rounded off degrees, count the number of degrees in between cusps.

From 7° to 30°   23°
       plus 1°   1°
                   _____

                    24°

Look up 24° in our table under "house size". On the 24° line, we find the "low point" number for this house size to be 14°45'.

We add this number 14°45
to the ascendant 7°06
the "low point" is 21°51 Leo

Mark this point on the outer edge of the horoscope form (we recommend a color key). We do this with all other houses to know the "low points" of the 12 houses.

2nd Example: 10th House

The MC (10th house cusp) of the example horoscope is 20 Aries. The 11th cusp is 10 Gemini. The house size is 50°.

10   +   30   +   10   = 50°

Aries   Taurus   Gemini

We find that 50 degrees in our table gives the "low point" of 30°45'. Since the signs of the zodiac contain only 30 degrees, we actually arrive at 20°45 of the *next* sign, Taurus.

Example horoscope MC	20°00 Aries
"low point" table	+ 30°45
	50°45
	− 30°00 (one sign, Aries)
"low point" in the 10th	20°45 Taurus
Sun in the horoscope	19°15 Taurus

The Sun is positioned 1° before the "low point" which we can consider a "low point Sun".

The calculation of the "invert point" is done in the same manner, except in the OPPOSITE direction.

THE THREE ZONES OF EACH HOUSE ACCORDING TO QUALITY
Cardinal   *Fixed*   *Mutable*

Naturally, the three points (house cusp, "invert point", "low point") not only work as points but as areas of influence according to motivational *quality*.

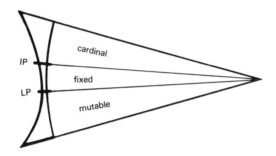

The impulse-giving energy of the *cardinal* cross corresponds to the area from the cusp of the house to the "invert point", the fixed and form giving phase of the fixed cross corresponds to the area from the "invert point" to the "low point". From the "low point" to the next house cusp corresponds with the mutable cross quality, the recognizing of new beginnings.

In this way, we can understand the "crisis mechanism" of the individual points, i.e. when a new quality begins, demanding adjustments to these different energy colorations.

At the house cusp, a change takes place insofar as, having reached a peak, it goes downhill again; the energies must be adjusted accordingly. At the "invert point", a viable form is created that is stabilized through the fixed quality. This form can not be allowed to become crystallized; it must remain viable. At the "low point", energies become quiet and relaxed, affording reflection and turn-around. There is the change from the fixed to the mutable, a new zone whose purpose is to overcome the restraining energies of the fixed zones, leading to the new house cusp with a new orientation.

The zones between these three points correspond to the three qualities and can be seen in the following breakdown:

House cusp	*to*	*"Invert point"*	*to*	*"Low point"*	*to*	*House cusp*
cardinal				fixed		mutable
performance				concentration		relaxation
energy				form		thought
exertion				collection		quiet
execution				consolidation		planning
creative process				utilization		thought creation

This list is only an outline; of course it can be easily expanded.

It is obvious that the three point-areas of a house take on additional different meanings depending upon the characterisitics of a cardinal, fixed, or mutable house. In each house, these points will be modified by the house theme. A "low point" in a *fixed* house, for example, will express a more typical perservering tendency than would happen in a mutable house where it will be less expressed. The "invert point" will function differently in a cardinal house than it will in a mutable house, and a house cusp in a cardinal house will be more strongly effective than in other houses, etc.

In this way, we have further divided the 12 houses into three zones each, resulting in 36 combination possibilities, offering more differentiated analysis of human behavior.

THE THREE-PHASE DEVELOPMENT PROCESSES OF THE HOROSCOPE

We can further appreciate the three qualities according to the formula "thought, energy, form".

In the mutable cross the thought is born	(thought)
In the cardinal cross comes impulse for action	(energy)
In the fixed cross form is added	(form)

This process is demonstrated with the following example:

Picture a potter making a vase. He takes the clay that is wet in order to begin forming it. This shaping process is done with vital energy, the kind indicated in the cardinal houses. When he is finished, he will be satisfied: he has created something and reached the perfect expression of what he has envisioned. He then lets the form dry before putting it in the kiln. This kiln makes the form hard and stable. The clay shrinks because the water evaporates. After the firing, the form is hard and stable and much less susceptible to destruction or negative processes. This form stabilization function is found in the fixed houses.

Each created and stabilized form is used for a purpose. We enjoy the use of it for a while, but one day perhaps we have the feeling: "it is not really so perfect; there is an imperfection; there is something that no longer meets my expectations".

Perhaps I am not satisfied any longer with the outer form, the aesthetic dimension. I begin to wonder how to make it better.

Such thoughts happen in the "recognition area" of the mutable houses. We ponder by becoming critical about what we have and we wonder if we can not improve things. Then we have an idea. By the time this idea consolidates, we have reached the next angle, a cardinal house. Here is the impulse to make something new of the idea which in the fixed cross then gains form and stability. In this example, the deeper meaning of the house system becomes clear: within the circle, the eternal change of life, the development and maturation of man is guaranteed. We can observe that process four times.

Let us demonstrate this in a "short formula".

In the 1st house	comes the impulse to create something useful to the "I."
In the 2nd house	we take possession of that creation and give form and stability to it.
In the 3rd house	we get to know the community and learn from it.
In the 4th house	we make ourselves at home within the community.
In the 5th house	we enjoy relationships to experience ourselves.
In the 6th house	we want to make things better because we know our weaknesses.
In the 7th house	comes the new impulse to relate to the YOU.
In the 8th house	we experience the partnership as part of the societal structure that regulates and protects things, and we recognize responsibilities.
In the 9th house	we strive toward freedom and develop ideas accordingly.
In the 10th house	we are sure of ourselves and want to lead others.
In the 11th house	we seek out others with our ideals and make them friends.
In the 12th house	we must say good-bye and part from everything in order to win a new focus.

Everything that lives goes through the three-phase process. Everywhere there is a certain process happening, be it in the mental, spiritual, or material sphere. There will first be the impulse to stimulate energy for action, followed by stabilization and then finally by enjoyment of the process. Later, we begin to recognize that something still better can be created, and the whole process starts all over again.

Everything man does is bound to this rhythm: creation, possession, utilization, enjoyment, then criticism, new plan and new creation.

All human behavior, human works, and relationships go through this process in this sequence. This is the actual evolutionary dynamic development force that governs all creative processes.

Psychological Horoscope Analysis

PRACTICAL ANALYSIS OF THE EXAMPLE HOROSCOPE

In conclusion, we want to discuss the example horoscope and its Sun and Moon positions as well as certain house influences that have to do with the development of self-awareness and with the themes of the 4th quadrant.

When we look at the chart (page 20), we see immediately that only one hemisphere is occupied by planets. The opposition of the 3/9 axis borders the YOU-side; the houses 4 to 8 will not weigh too heavily in the interests of the personality-development. This border axis functions at the same time as a selective barrier or a filter, only admitting people who meet the ideal conceptions of the Moon-Neptune axis position and the 4th quadrant (houses 10, 11 and 12).

The main planetary pattern is decidedly in the 4th quadrant, the BEING quadrant, that strives toward conscious self-realization and "I"-formation, always aligning itself with inner ideals. The Moon-Neptune opposition in the thought axis acts as a barrier to the other planets. This indicates an introverted base of consciousness.

This human being is predominantly interested in mental things. The concentration of planets around the 11th cusp suggests humanitarian endeavors, progressive ideas, and an idealized image of man.

The Sun, positioned in the earth sign Taurus, open to material enjoyments, is held back at the "low point" and, additionally, plays a smaller role due to its relatively unattached position within the whole aspect picture. This can present a problem. Unaspected planets work out as "independent mechanisms" when they are not recognized in their functioning capacity. Since the Sun is the central organ of self-awareness, we would want to take a closer look:

The Sun is positioned at the "low point" in the 10th house in Taurus.

From earlier discussions, we know what the sun in the 10th house means: that it wants to be a self-confident personality and recognized as such by others. The Sun strives for a position in the world.

The Sun at the "low point" will not be able to do this. Exterior opportunities for assertion appear denied; self-confidence can not outwardly express itself. This human being lives more within himself; his inner being will be falsely evaluated by the exterior value-system. Also, the Sun is only weakly connected in the aspect picture by a sextile to the Moon. The Sun can not be activated from the consciousness, from the "inner blueprint". Physically, this can indicate a weak constitution.

From a psychological point of view, the Sun's unrelatedness within the aspect picture suggests a danger of being unduly influenced and directed by the environment, at least in younger years or until a development process is recognized within.

The environment demands from the "10th house Sun" a personal stand, an individual format. The position in the individuality sphere points toward a striving upward, the "low point" indicates development of inner, human values. The expression that must be found is the development of inner values and one's own Being.

This person will have to give up ambitious goals and personal authority needs in favor of inner maturation.

Even though the Sun's sign, Taurus, measures the self-worth in possessions of material or mental abilities or in talents, life here asks to forego material success and concentrate on spiritual, inner values. The *sign* Taurus, like the Sun, also finds itself in a "closed in" position: it does not occupy a house cusp! As we recall, the energies of a sign are applied through the house cusps into practical life. The tendency of Taurus to accumulate substance should, in this case, be applied less to exterior life and more to the inner stratum. This inner development must be recognized and accepted first.

Through the unaspected Sun, this human being will be influenced and motivated by the environment to make it in the world, to rise above the masses to a special status (10th house). He will surely try everything possible to meet the expectations of the parents (Sun and Saturn high in the horoscope). But he will be successful only to a certain degree.

The parents expect something special from him but, at the same time, make the mistake of suppressing his self-esteem. They have projected into the child their own hopes to amount to something in the world. But the child can not fulfill these hopes because they do not correspond with his own natural predisposition. It is of special importance for parents and educators to recognize the real abilities of any child, to support these abilities and give up conscious or sub-conscious projective demands.

With parental expectations maintained, serious inner crises and exterior professional difficulties can result (10th house; profession). The vital Sun energies are directed inward. When the demands from the environment become too great for these energies, they jam up and can stagnate. This can lead to behavioral overcompensation when outer pressure becomes too strong. Pluto on the Ascendant will be used as this compensation for self-esteem in a demonstrative need to impress (Leo). Since Pluto is still *before the ascendant* in the passive 12th house, it can not be maintained in the long run.

Inferiority or superiority complexes can develop interchangeably, giving the overall impression that the person is something very special but not recognized as such by others. Such steady frustration can lead to guilt feelings and corresponding depression, making harmonious development difficult or even impossible. It's crucial for parents to recognize the child's real predisposition and encourage it.

Analysis of *the Moon* now becomes important. Positioned on the 9th house cusp, it *can* develop outwardly. It can reach the environment and be accepted. There *is* possibility here of developing the self.

In the combination of Sun and Moon, we recognize that this person is able to realize himself more in self-feeling (Moon) than in self-awareness (Sun). Self-realization, individuation, can not happen through the Sun; it must be mainly realized through the Moon. Practically speaking, an ambitious materialistic goal should not be strived for; rather, a more serving, helping work chosen, according the the Pisces Moon and the humanitarian ideals of the BEING quadrant.

Essential facts here are that the 9th house cusp begins a flexible house and the Moon is in a mutable sign (Pisces): the combination of house and sign here is practicable. Predisposition and environmental situation are in harmony.

The 9th house requires its own thought processes; the gist of problems must be recognized, and inner goal orientation must be found through personal reflection. The "devoted" sign Pisces easily adjusts to such circumstances, and the Moon instinctively does the same.

This Moon position indicates that the personal thinking process has an instinctive grasp for truth, that this will be brought into conscious confrontation with collective thinking. The opposition in the thinking axis between the Moon and Neptune makes it extremely difficult to assert the self against collective ideals. Disappointments, doubts about the self and the world, fear of public opinion and of what others say, and, most of all, the fear that one's own ideals are disrespected and undervalued must be experienced and suffered before they are mentally processed and matured into personal understanding.

The Moon is positioned deepest into the YOU-hemisphere. As a contact body and through the sign Pisces, there is a strong indication of a need for love and understanding. The Moon, by its position on the right side will be much "exploited". In Pisces, the Moon is sensitive, waiting and receptive. The Moon is easily influenced by the YOU and exposed to its evaluation. That is why this person wants to adjust to the environment and in good faith do what is asked of him. Out of this wish to "do good" a whole philosophy is born (9th house).

The opposition in the thought axis between the Moon and Neptune points to an acute problem in the thinking process, and the solution must be found in the existence axis, 6/12. The focus upon inner, spiritual values and the tendency to idealization (as well as the wish to adjust) from the Moon must be applied constructively so that there is no chance to develop a gap between reality and idealism. A gap could lead to an illusionary world in isolation and loneliness.

This person would then greatly suffer because of his needs for contact and love.

The special abilities and, with them, the solution to the problems are in a serving and healing dimension, one that must be recognized vocationally. The "third pole" in the present axis problem is in the existence axis and suggests through Mars in Cancer on the 12th house cusp a helping vocation in hospitals or institutions. In a female horoscope the profession of a nurse comes to mind; in a male horoscope, work with retarded children.

The social and helping tendencies are confirmed also by Venus. Venus also is in the 9th house and at the "invert point" at that, indicating the best way to use productive energies successfully in life.

In conclusion, we can say that the strong needs for self-realization and individuation, indicated by the Sun in the BEING quadrant, the planetary concentration in the same area, the Moon at the 9th house cusp, and the Leo ascendant, are best expressed through service to others. Such work will lead to an inner self-awareness that can exist independent of the opinion of others and can follow securely and with determination the true calling. In this way, this human being can be a fountain of strength and inner support to others, which for him is his best self-fulfillment.

We can see how a horoscope shows a weakness in one position and a solution in other areas. The knowledge of these possibilities puts man in the position to solve his problems, avoiding difficulties or detours in his development. The horoscope becomes a valuable therapeutic tool: it shows us the path toward self-realization and self-development.

Of course, nothing has been yet introduced in this example analysis dealing with *individual* planetary and sign influences. There will be another volume to follow this one, in this series *ASTROLOGICAL PSYCHOLOGY*, that will deal with aspect structures. Only then will a full analysis of the individual and his behavior's psychological fine points be possible. We have limited ourselves in this volume to the houses, to show how to use the house system practically. We see how we can deduct vitally important behavioral factors from the patters of house activation. Truly, man begins to find himself when he is aware of the world around him.

Index

A Selection of Weiser Publications . . .

Other Books on the Huber Method

Lifeclock: The Huber Method of Timing in the Horoscope

Originally published in two volumes, this work was reissued in 1994 as one volume.

"*Lifeclock* simply and clearly explains the authors' theory of age progression. Tested and proved. . .through years of research, and backed up by their two decades of experience in psychological counseling, the age-progression technique is a way of determining where we are in life and how we can make the best of current influences in light of problems past, present, or future. . . .This is a technique for symbolically representing inner development rather than outer circumstances. . . .If you're in search of an astrological tool for determining where you are in life's journey, *Life Clock* is worth investigating."   —*Horoscope*

"This is a book for all counseling astrologers to read carefully and apply to their chosen delineation methods. It can do nothing but enhance the ability to understand humankind. Well-written and illustrated."
                              —*Astro-Analysis Publications Newsletter*

"This is an excellent book written by two excellent astrologers. . . .For those of you who have never tried to work with the Age Point, you might be in for an exciting adventure. . . It is another symbolic way of advancing the chart, and it works uncannily well."
                                                        —*Mercury Hour*

"a clear explanation of Huber's Age Point Method. . . .The diagrams and presentations are first class. "   — *Considerations*

• • • • • • •

Moon Node Astrology

Currently a best-seller in German, this is Louise and Bruno Huber's latest book. The English translation will be available in 1995.

Also of Interest

Seminars in Psychological Astrology Series by Dr. Liz Greene and Howard Sasportas.

Dr. Liz Greene and Howard Sasportas are co-founders of the Centre for Psychological Astrology in England. Dr. Liz Greene is a Jungian analyst and practicing astrologer who lives outside of London. Until his death in May 1992, Howard Sasportas was a practicing astrologer and psychotherapist, trained in humanistic psychology and psychosynthesis.

The Development of Personality, Volume 1 discusses how early traumas and experiences affect the development of individual identity. This book focuses on psychological complexes and astrological factors that encompass issues from childhood, including, subpersonalities, the stages of childhood, the parental marriage and puer and senex.

14.95

Dynamics of the Unconscious, Volume 2 sheds light on the darker side of adult personality, those unconscious dynamics you need to confront to grow. Through the symbolism of astrology, psychology, and alchemy, the authors show you how to understand depression, aggression, and the quest for the sublime.

The Luminaries: The Psychology of the Sun and Moon in the Horoscope, Volume 3 is an extensive exploration of the Sun and Moon, and how they symbolize the psychological development of the individual. The authors discuss the mythology and psychology of the Moon and its relevance as a significator of relationships. The correspondence between the Sun and the development of the consciousness is explored in depth.

The Inner Planets, Volume 4 discusses the value of Mercury, Venus, and Mars as they symbolize important aspects of personality. This book is about the process of understanding how the inner planets actually represent the individual, and how they directly color the energy of the Sun and Moon.

Other Books by Dr. Liz Greene

Astrology for Lovers

The Astrology of Fate

Relating: An Astrological Guide
to Living with Others on a Small Planet

Saturn: A New Look at an Old Devil

Astrology World Congress

Every year the Hubers co-organize and lecture at the Astrology World Congress held in Lucerne, Switzerland. The Congress is a four day conference that brings together world renowned astrological authors and consultants from many countries to share their experiences and expertise. With over 70 lectures and workshops—offered in both German and English—the Congress offers an invaluable overview of modern astrology and its application in various fields, including education, psychology, health care, politics, and commerce. For both the student and professional astrologer, this conference provides a unique opportunity to participate in an international exchange of ideas, and the chance to learn from prominent and accomplished experts the latest methods of astrological interpretation, counseling and therapy techniques.

For more information about attending this Astrology World Congress write to:

Verkehrsverein Luzern
Haldenstrasse 6
CH-6002 Luzern
Switzerland

About the Institute

The Hubers founded the Astrological Psychology Institute (API) in Adliswil/Zürich, Switzerland in 1962. They started by providing astrological character analysis by mail and individual therapy. Personally trained in Florence by Dr. Robert Assagioli, the founder of psychosynthesis, the Hubers incorporated this experience into their curriculum and therapy, as well as their own discovery during their study in Florence involving the use of color-dialogue to treat therapy blocks. They developed this technique into a color-psychological concept applicable to the astrological chart. In 1968 they began offering the public courses in astrological psychology. The courses were so popular that the institute quickly expanded. In 1974 they began a formal two-year training program for counselors and therapists. By 1977 they had over 2000 students and were conducting summer courses all over Germany and year-long classes in three Swiss cities. They now have a school in Devon, England, known as the English Huber School. Highly regarded worldwide as a serious astrological school with professional standards, the Huber School now offers a correspondence course that teaches the Huber-Method to students all over the world. Annually at the institute in Zürich the Hubers offer the API Diploma Seminar.

For more information about API in Switzerland write to:

Astrologisch-Psychologisches Institut
Postfach 614
Obertilistrasse 4
CH-8134 Adliswil
Zürich
Switzerland

For more information about the Huber School in England write to:

The English Huber School
PO Box 118
Knutsford
Cheshire WA16 8TG
England

For over thirty years Louise and Bruno Huber have been working with astrological psychology—teaching, training, and writing. They are the founders of the internationally recognized Astrological Psychology Institute (API) in Adliswil/Zürich, Switzerland, and the English Huber School in Devon, England. In addition to personal counseling practices, the Hubers teach at both schools, and lecture all over the world. For the past several years they have been keynote speakers at the American Federation of Astrologers Convention and since 1981 they have been co-organizers of the now-famous international World Congress in Astrology held every year in Lucerne, Switzerland. They are the authors of several books including three volumes in their *Astrological Psychology Series.*